Nexus 10 Guide

Master Your Tablet in Just One Evening

Erik Marcus

Mocana Productions Incorporated

For Joshua Warchol

Contents

Acknowledgments

I gratefully acknowledge Drew Mitty and Karen Jones for helping to copyedit this text. I am additionally indebted to Diane Koerber Miller for catching a number of mistakes that occurred during typesetting and eBook conversion. Finally, I thank Venkatesh Rao for his encouraging words as I embarked upon this project.

Introduction

Amazing things happen when a technology giant decides to dominate five key areas of its industry, and is willing to pour virtually unlimited amounts of money into coming out on top.

Over the past decade, Google has sought to produce the computer industry's best web browser (Chrome), email service (Gmail), office software (Google Docs), and cloud-based file storage.

As if this weren't ambitious enough for one company, Google has also spent billions of dollars to create its very own operating system, Android, which has by all accounts blossomed into a worthy competitor to the operating systems created by Apple and Microsoft.

Is Android plus Google's slate of tools the absolute best solution for every possible need? For many people the answer is already an emphatic yes. And it's simply beyond dispute that Google's offerings are collectively so good as to be breathtaking. These are powerful, beautifully refined tools that you could fall in love with.

Nexus tablets are the culmination of all of Google's efforts over the past five years. They're designed to be the single best tablet and smart phone devices for Google's interlocking collection of applications and services.

Thanks to Android's exquisitely refined touch screen interface, the Nexus 10 is simultaneously one of the most versatile and easy-to-use computing devices ever created. It approaches the gold standard set by the iPad in terms of polish, power, and usability—exceeding the iPad in some respects, coming up short in others, but making an admirable showing in every key area. What's more, the Android operating system at the heart of the Nexus 10 is constantly improving, which means that over time the Nexus 10 will only get more powerful and satisfying to use. For Nexus 10 owners, all of these forthcoming upgrades will be installed automatically and for free.

The experience of using the Nexus 10 is already so seamless that the primary challenge involves understanding the multitude of ways this tablet can improve your life. And that's where this book comes in. Read this book and within hours you'll know how to accomplish things with your tablet that, just a few years ago, were impossible for anyone but highly-trained computer experts.

There's a lot to learn, but none of it is boring and very little of it is technical or difficult to understand. So let's get started!

Chapter 1

The First Five Things

Let's get some quick and basic one-time setup tasks out of the way so you can begin putting your Nexus 10 to full use. Ten minutes spent doing these things will make your Nexus 10 vastly more powerful for the rest of its life with you.

1) Log in to your wireless network.

Touch the Apps Screen button in your dock (the Apps Screen button is in the Dock's center showing a circle containing six squares). You'll be taken to the Apps Screen, where you should then touch the icon for the Settings app. The very first option on the Setting app's screen is Wi-Fi. Drag the Wi-Fi switch to the On position if Wi-Fi is not already on. Then touch the Wi-Fi menu item. This will bring up a screen showing the local wireless networks currently available. Select the network you want and, if you are prompted to do so, enter your wireless network's password.

You can follow these steps whenever you visit a coffeehouse or airport and need to log into a new wireless network.

2) Sign in to Gmail, if you haven't already done so.

When you ordered your Nexus 10, you had the chance to input your Gmail or Google Apps-powered email address. If you provided this address, your Nexus 10 ships with access to your Gmail, calendar, and other Google services all set to go. You'll just need to enter your password once.

If your Nexus 10 does not have your Google account preloaded, open the Settings app, scroll down to Accounts, and touch *+ Add account.* Touch the *Google* option in the popup window and then type your Gmail or Google Apps email address and your password.

You can also enter a Microsoft Exchange-powered email address by touching the Corporate button on this popup menu, or you can select the *Email* option to give your Nexus 10 access to a competing email service like Hotmail or Yahoo Mail.

If you don't currently have a Gmail account or an email address powered by Google Apps, I urge you to get one right away. This will open the door to Google's entire range of cloud-based apps and services. And while you can certainly use your Nexus 10 without a Google account, your device will be crippled in many important ways. Much of this book is devoted to teaching you to take advantage of the numerous services that Google bundles with each account. Since you have already invested in a Nexus 10, and a Gmail address is free, you would be nuts not to sign up for an account so that you can get full use out of your Nexus 10.

You'll now be forever signed in to your Nexus 10 and the entire suite of Google's services unless you deliberately sign out. What do I mean by Google's entire suite of services? I mean you get access to all sorts of vital stuff, from your Gmail to live bookmarks to an entire collection of free Student and Office productivity apps, with full cloud-based collaboration abilities built into every app.

3) Sign into the Chrome browser on your desktop or laptop.

Sign in by opening Chrome on your desktop or laptop, and then select *Sign into Chrome...* from beneath the *Chrome* menu.

Assuming you're now signed in to your Nexus 10 (You already did this in Step 2) you'll now have immediate access to all your Mac or PC's bookmarks on your Nexus 10. If you're not currently using Chrome as your primary browser on your desktop or laptop, consider exporting bookmarks from whatever browser you're using, and importing them into Chrome.

The Nexus 10's version of Chrome is stripped down to the point that I don't like using it to bookmark websites. Instead, I use my Nexus 10 to visit bookmarks I've already created through Chrome on my desktop computer.

4) Grab a few games.

Go to the Play Store store by touching the shopping bag icon in the Dock. Then touch the Apps button, and then the Games button. Drag your finger from right to left to see the various lists of games. You'll start with a screen showing featured games, then you'll see the top paid games, and then the top free games.

If you want to search for games by title touch the magnifying glass and type in the name of the game you're seeking.

You can't go wrong starting out with Angry Birds, Flick Golf, or Age of Zombies. If thinking games are more your style, there are great versions of solitaire and sudoku available.

5) Customize your Home screen.

Why settle for factory defaults? Your Nexus 10 doesn't truly become yours until you've set up your Home screen just the way you like it. Complete directions are laid out in Chapter 8.

Get started now by changing to a custom wallpaper. Just hold your finger down on any spot of the Home screen that's not occupied by a widget or app icon, and a wallpaper selection popup menu will appear.

Chapter 2

Why Tablets?

Around 2000, many computer users began switching from desktops to laptops. And today, far more laptops are sold than desktops. But the rise of laptops wasn't revolutionary. A laptop is nothing more than a desktop shrunk down to a portable form. Little else changes: it's got the same ports, the same operating system, and the same software.

By contrast, in both hardware and software, today's tablets represent a total rethink of the desktop and laptop era. And as with every revolutionary idea, tablets were widely misunderstood at the beginning.

When the iPad first hit, some critics (wrongfully, it turns out) wrote off these devices as perfectly fine for consuming text and media, but lousy for creating stuff or getting any meaningful work done. It turns out, however, that tablets are amazing work tools—they can be *much* better for some jobs than a Mac or Windows PC. That's not to say that tablets can replace a PC in every situation. There are still many cases where a PC is the ideal or only solution. But tablets are rapidly becoming the best platform for a wide range of tasks.

In fact, many people can get by exclusively with tablets. For instance, my mother uses her tablet daily, yet she never touches the family's Mac—since there's nothing she needs to do that can't be done on her tablet. She can access everything she wants on her tablet, handle her email perfectly, and even send airline boarding passes and whatnot straight to the printer.

So far I've established that tablets are wonderful for some tasks, and can even meet many people's entire computing needs. But I still haven't gotten to their most valuable quality: they enable you to consume information and media in a remarkably more relaxing and enjoyable way than if you had used a conventional PC.

Here's the delightful thing about tablets. You'll find that the way you engage with them enables you to be vastly more relaxed than you are when you're using a PC. Why is this so important? Let me give you one example. Any frequent computer user has, at some point, encountered a long document online that deserved a careful read. And that moment, when you're using a PC, is always a tremendous drag. That's because reading any lengthy document on a PC is fundamentally unpleasant. At best (in the most ergonomic setting possible), you're stuck in an office chair while you glue your eyes to the monitor on your desk. In fact, many PC users go through the hassle, expense, and waste of printing long articles and documents so that they won't be forced to read them online.

But on a tablet, everything changes. You can be on your living room couch, hanging out at a coffee shop, or even snuggled up in bed—and thoroughly enjoy your reading experience. No PC lets you consume books, music, or video in such comfort.

Why is a tablet so much more comfortable? Because you can hold it right in your hands. By holding it in your hands, the tablet tends to be much closer to your eyes, so you see everything more clearly and with less eyestrain. And since you can sit however you'd like (or even lie down), your body can be a lot more relaxed and comfortable.

I can't adequately stress the importance of this added relaxation. How are you supposed to interact with your information in a positive and productive way if your body is stressed while you're taking it in? Suddenly, thanks to the invention of tablets, your main portal to the world of information and online interaction is accessible away from the dreaded office chair.

So this key portion of your life, in which you're using the Internet to explore information or to connect with people, is suddenly offered to you in a way that permits relaxed interaction. That can open the door to some remarkable benefits. This book is devoted primarily to exploring how to use your tablet to bring as much to your life as possible.

So what can I do with my Nexus 10?

A Nexus 10 is undeniably portable, but what the heck can you use it for?

To start, your Nexus 10 is in many respects the ideal device for accessing the Internet. It features the latest version of Google's Chrome browser, which means that it's capable of delivering the web's most advanced features.

Without getting too technical, the World Wide Web has evolved to enable you to do all sorts of things that were once possible using only stand-alone apps. By using a modern browser like Chrome, you can use interactive websites to play games, handle your to-do lists, do your taxes, and stream music.

Many internet-based services allow you to choose between accessing them through Chrome via a website, or through a custom app downloaded from the Google Play store. For instance, you can stream songs through Pandora on Chrome, but you can also access the service by installing the Pandora app.

Current web standards allow developers to accomplish a heck of a lot by building websites for Chrome. But the best websites still can't measure up to the best "native" apps (a native app is coded specifically for a given operating system, and thereby gains access to abilities that web-based standards don't yet offer.) As a result, generally speaking, apps downloaded from Google Play tend to offer a richer experience than do their web-based counterparts. Sometimes the difference in quality is tiny, while in others cases it's immense.

In nearly every situation in which a website is available for Android as a native app, the app will offer a better experience than the website. So if there's a web-based service you especially enjoy, search Google Play to find out if the company that owns the website has also created an app by the same name. As one example, you can certainly do your taxes this year by using the Chrome web browser to interact with the TurboTax.com website. But you'll probably find that the TurboTax app available through Google Play is an all-around better solution than the web-based version.

That said, I wouldn't want to do my taxes on a Nexus 10—I'd want the larger screen of a desktop. This book is all about using the right tool for the right job.

You'll probably wind up using your Nexus 10 in four ways. You'll be using it to:

- Manage your life: access your email, calendars, to-do lists, and more.

- Use Chrome to browse the web.

- Download apps from Google Play: games, productivity software, and drawing tools are just the start of what's available.

- Access a full range of digital media, including movies, music, newspapers, books, and magazines.

Owning both the Nexus 7 and the Nexus 10, I tend to view the latter as a Lincoln Town Car. It's too big to be worth taking out of the garage for five minute trips to town, but it's super comfy for long drives. When I want to do extended reading sessions or watch a movie, I appreciate the Nexus 10's extra size, its better speakers, and its sharper screen. By contrast, if I just want to give a quick glance at email or the weather report, I'll generally pick up my Nexus 7.

Here are the sorts of things I do most often with my Nexus 10:

- Using Instapaper to send long articles from my desktop to my Nexus 10 for reading at my leisure.

- Reading books via the Kindle or Play Books apps.

- Texting and video chats via the Talk app.

- Using Gmail or Google's calendar. I still prefer a desktop or laptop for these tasks, but for briefly checking my email or calendar the Nexus 10 works great.

- Timer and Alarm Clock apps. These are ridiculously simple apps, but I use them constantly.

- Playing podcasts. Once you discover the universe of podcasts, commercial radio will lose all appeal.

- YouTube. Sure, I'd rather watch a long YouTube video on my desktop, but I find myself playing short YouTube videos on my Nexus 10 all the time.

- Light gaming. For hard-core First Person Shooters and the like, desktops and game consoles remain the platforms of choice.

- Voice Search. Anytime I need to know something that a minimally competent person would be capable of quickly looking up online, I just touch the microphone button on the Home screen and ask the Voice Search. Most of the time, she'll have my answer in seconds.

All in all, you're likely to use your Nexus 10 for a much wider range of activities than you ever imagined when you purchased your device. There are a few great iPad apps—Tweetbot, Mr. Reader, and IA Writer—that I wish had equally superb Nexus 10 counterparts. But lately, I've found that I'm no longer picking up my iPad except for when I need to use those apps. My Nexus 10 gives me everything I need. I also expect that, in short order, the Nexus 10 will have a few killer apps that you can't get on the iPad.

I hope this book helps you to get as much as possible out of your Nexus 10. Please keep in mind that this book is about teaching you all that you can do with your Nexus 10. If you are seeking step-by-step instructions for performing basic tasks on your tablet visit Nexus10Guide.com to check out my free video tutorials.

Chapter 3

Understanding Cloud Computing

Chances are that you're reading this because you just purchased a Nexus 10. If so, you've made a fantastic choice. It's a remarkably powerful tablet that compares favorably to the iPad in just about every important respect.

The iPad was released in April of 2010, and became an instant runaway success. Over the next two years, Apple sold more than 67 million iPads worldwide. Windows PC makers viewed the iPad's success as a mortal threat, and virtually every major hardware manufacturer rushed competing tablets to market. Every single one of these tablets was mediocre at best, and laughably inferior to the iPad. The main reason why competing tablets couldn't measure up is that most were built on Android 2.x and 3.x, an operating system that lacked the performance, polish, and design quality of iOS (the operating system at the heart of the iPad and iPhone).

But in late 2011 Google released Android 4.0, which for the first time put Android in the same league as iOS. And in June of 2012, Google followed up 4.0 by baking a boatload of refinements into the "Jelly Bean" 4.1 version of Android, which offered serious performance and user interface improvements. Now, with the release of

Android 4.2, the Nexus 10 offers a user experience of comparable elegance to the iOS operating system at the heart of Apple's iPad.

As this book will convincingly demonstrate, the Nexus 10 is a better choice than the iPad in several important respects. What's more, the Nexus 10 blows the iPad out of the water in terms of value. You get a tablet with a slick, beautifully designed interface. It's got built-in voice recognition and a Voice Search that are comparable to what Apple's Siri can offer. And even in its early days, many of the best and most useful iPad apps are available in excellent versions on Android.

The point of this book is to get you acquainted with the primary capabilities of your Nexus 10, and to show you how to get the most from your new tablet. If you've never owned a tablet before I've got good news for you: your Nexus 10 is vastly easier to learn and to master than any laptop or desktop computer you've ever used—Macs and Windows machines alike.

Tablets are easier to use than PCs for two main reasons. First, an interface that allows you to directly touch icons and interact with apps with your fingertip is intrinsically easier to understand and use than one that is mouse-driven. Second, tablet operating systems have done away with the standard disk hierarchy system of traditional Macs and PCs. It turns out that most computer users have an easy time learning just about any sort of software, except for understanding file systems and disk hierarchies. So with both Android and iOS, your data is saved in a very simplified cloud storage system, where the apps take care of where everything is placed.

So what does this mean, in practice? If I'm editing this book on my Macintosh, and relying on its file system rather than the cloud for storage, here is the folder hierarchy of where my book file lives:

```
MacintoshHD>Users>Erik>Documents>Nexus10Book>Guide.RTF
```

To navigate to that file on a Mac, I must understand the above hierarchy. And understanding this hierarchy involves at least partially grasping some fairly difficult concepts that are at the heart of how modern desktop operating systems are organized.

By contrast, here is where my book exists on my Google Drive:

```
Nexus10Book>Guide.RTF
```

See what's going on here? Using Google Drive, you don't need to understand a complex disk hierarchy in order to know where your files are kept. They're actually being stored somewhere out on the cloud, but you need not know exactly where. The documents component of Google Drive sweats the details of knowing where to find your word processing files.

Cloud Backups

We've just seen that Android automatically circumvents forcing its users to navigate the complex world of file hierarchies, which is the single most baffling part of the operating system for inexperienced users. The responsibility of dealing with file hierarchies is handed off to app developers, for whom the task of dealing with basic file management is child's play.

But you might ask, "If I'm not going to be responsible for navigating a file system's hierarchy, where will my files actually live?"

The answer to this question is, "On the cloud."

So you might then respond, "Well then, what does 'on the cloud' mean?"

And one valid answer might be, "It means: don't worry about it. Everything's taken care of."

But suppose you wanted to press a little more, and were determined to find out where the heck your photos, word processing documents, contact information, and calendar dates actually reside.

In nearly all cases on the Nexus 10, this and other information is stored, as I said, on "the cloud." And on Android devices, this typically means that your various apps have saved your files to one of the countless Google-owned servers scattered across the Internet. It would take a professional server administrator to determine where each of these files actually live. It might be, for instance, that the Google Docs file of your letter to your uncle lives at one of the thousands of PCs humming at the Google server farm in Bend, Oregon. The photo you took of your dog, by contrast, may well be stored at another Google server farm in Texas. But you don't need to know any of this, since each app takes care of storing, updating, and retrieving files that live on the cloud.

You might as well also know that no one company owns "the cloud"—it's a generic term for online data storage, in which the user doesn't have to keep track of servers and disk hierarchies. So if you're an iPad user, most of your documents and photos may also be stored on the cloud—but in this case the servers will be generally be located at Apple's various server farms. Once again, the user doesn't need to know or care where these files go; in each case the dirty work of navigating the storage or retrieval of a given file is handled by the app that created it.

If, as I do, you use non-google Web services like Twitter or Pinboard.in or Instagram, your data is once again being saved to the cloud, often to servers owned by Amazon.com.

When it comes to locating your files, the cloud makes everything simple by eliminating your need to navigate complex file hierarchies to save or retrieve data. It's safe to say that millions of person-hours have been wasted over the years by people trying to locate files they have lost somewhere in disk hierarchies whose structure they only vaguely understand.

Speaking of lost files, this brings us to the ultimate computer disaster: hard disk crashes. See, until the rise of cloud computing, most people were storing their precious photos, music, spreadsheets, and other files on the hard drives inside their desktops and laptops.

A hard disk spins at about 7200 rotations per minute, with its magnetic head hovering just nanometers above the disk. This incredibly delicate design is obviously prone to failure. Hard drives are one of the miracles of the information age, but they're also the most fragile part of any computer system. These drives can and do go bad, and there's rarely any warning before they fail. If your drive crashes and you haven't been backing up to another drive, you've likely just lost everything if you don't resort to unreliable, inconvenient, and expensive recovery methods.

Some of the most traumatic moments in people's lives been occurred as a result of hard disk crashes. Novels and dissertations lost, precious photographs destroyed, vital business information and tax data all out the window.

So ever since the invention of spinning disk media, the mantra of every computer savvy person has always been to have multiple backups. The trouble is that these backups are also being made on failure-prone spinning disk media. And it's one thing to purchase an extra backup drive (or two), but quite another to have a system in place where things properly get backed up. If you're writing a book and haven't backed up in two weeks and your computer hard drive suddenly suffers a head crash, you've just lost two weeks' worth of work plus who knows what else.

Now if you're a Mac or PC user you could read some articles on data integrity and institute a backup scheme just like what the pros do. In my case, for nearly 20 years, this has involved the hassle of buying an extra hard drive and keeping it at my parents' house. And while I've no doubt that my personal back-up system is head-and-shoulders above the average person's, it's still pathetic when compared to the best practices of professional server administrators. If my house burns to cinders, any data I've stored since the last time I took my backup drive to my parents' house is gone forever.

All of this brings us to the next great advantage of cloud storage. Whether your data is being uploaded to a part of the cloud owned by Google or Amazon or Apple, you can feel confident knowing these companies employ the world's best server administrators to carry out constant backups. Once your files and data are on the cloud, the chances of their being lost is about as close to nil as you can possibly get.

We've now seen that the cloud not only bypasses your need to learn about file system navigation, it also lifts the annoying and surprisingly complex burden of data backups from your shoulders.

That said, files are precious and storage is so cheap it's practically free. An extra local backup never hurts, even if your data lives on the cloud. For instance, as I work on this book I'm saving the main file to my Google Drive. Yet even though the draft of this book lives safely on Google's cloud, I make a point each day to back up the latest version of my book from my Google Drive to my Mac's hard drive.

The fact that the Nexus 10 is based on cloud computing means it's easier to use than desktops, and your data is more reliably safeguarded against loss. But there's yet another strong advantage your Nexus 10 has over traditional desktops, and that concerns its protection against viruses.

The Story of Viruses

Even 112-year-old great grandmothers living in Upper Volta have heard of computer viruses and the damage they cause. But on your Nexus 10, you need not give viruses a thought. The story behind how the virus problem was solved on tablet devices is interesting, and easy for a non-technical person to understand.

Unfortunately, as we are about to see, the approach taken by Apple and Google to lock out viruses has also given these companies unprecedented abilities to lock out competitors. This may be good for Apple and Google, but it's not good for users of their tablets. In fact, a big part of why the Nexus 10 was created is that Google realized that Apple would never grant iPad users full access to Google's suite of apps and services. But I'm now getting ahead of myself; let's begin this overview with a look at the origin of computer viruses.

The virus concept was first described in a 1972 academic paper. But it was not until the early 1990s that the threat of viruses became serious and widespread. The height of Microsoft's Windows dominance, spanning roughly from the Windows 95 to XP releases, was an especially bad time. Viruses were by then everywhere and the protections against them were clumsy and often expensive.

A virus is a tiny piece of self-replicating code attached to a software application. Perhaps the most common way that a virus creator spreads his pernicious creation is to attach it to a pirated game or productivity application, and then upload that file to a website hosting pirated software.

Once you download a piece of compromised software and run it, the software might spread to other programs, which, if shared, would infect other people's computers.

As software coding challenges go, writing a simple virus is one of the easiest projects possible. There's not much of anything to a virus—they're often just a couple dozen lines of code. Since the bar to coding viruses is so low, this has opened the door to thousands of viruses being created worldwide by criminals, bored teenagers, and sociopaths.

In Windows, the dominant method to shield computers from viruses involves adding an extension to the operating system that scans any new program the very first time it's about to be run. These antivirus programs work by comparing the contents of a new application against a database of known viruses.

The problem with this method is that since new viruses are always being written, the antivirus software's database must be kept current at all times—if you download a three-day-old virus and your antivirus software's database was last updated a week ago, you're hosed.

At this point, you can see that the only way to keep viruses at bay on the desktop, at least on Windows machines during the 1990s, was to rely on a constantly-updated virus checker. Unfortunately, we now smack into a bit of computer history that caused the task of shielding Windows computers from viruses to be needlessly expensive and full of hassle. It's all related to the fact that Windows 95 was so extraordinarily successful as to essentially give Microsoft a monopoly of the personal computing industry. The company was raking in gobs of money from sales of its operating system as well as its hugely overpriced office software. So much cash was being generated that even Microsoft's low-level administrative staff were becoming stock millionaires.

The U.S. government generally frowns on monopolies. So while Microsoft of that era had no reason to fear Apple, they had every reason to fear the feds, who could easily break up the company just like they did to AT&T back in the 1980s.

Well, what does any of this have to do with antivirus software? Let's get back to that point.

Microsoft knew that in order to preserve its extraordinarily profitable operating system and office software monopolies, it couldn't do anything to antagonize the feds and invite prosecution under the Sherman Antitrust Act. So when it came to the issue of virus protection, Microsoft decided to throw its own customers under the bus.

Here's what was going on: for a company as huge as Microsoft, building an industry-leading antivirus system into Windows would have cost peanuts. Creating this virus protection would have been so cheap that Microsoft could have afforded to give it away for free as part of the Windows operating system.

The trouble was that by the time viruses became a legitimate threat worthy of Microsoft taking the time to address, several cruddy little antivirus companies had emerged. If Microsoft had rendered these third-party offerings irrelevant by bundling antivirus protection into Windows, these antivirus companies would have gone crying to the feds.

So even though bundling virus protection into Windows was obviously the right thing to do, Microsoft was not about to do anything that would put its Windows and office suite monopolies at risk of being gutted by antitrust litigation.

As a corporation, Microsoft's primary responsibility was to its shareholders—not its customers. So to protect its core business, Microsoft turned its back on its own customers when it came to virus protection. If you wanted virus protection—something that shifted from desirable to essential as the 1990s wore on—you'd have to buy antivirus software from one of these third party software companies. These antivirus companies were—and still are—crappy companies one and all. Nearly every single one of these companies bases its business model on the fact that antivirus software must be constantly updated in order to provide adequate protection. So they either sell you their software or give it away for free, but in order for it to keep working you have to pay a yearly subscription fee of $30 to $50. And none of these companies feel any misgivings when it comes to tying your system up with all sorts of nagging dialog boxes. These antivirus systems are often deliberately difficult to uninstall, and if you ever stop paying your subscription fee you will get barraged by unending nag screens every time you turn on your computer.

So basically, as a Windows user after 1995, you had a horrible choice. You could either go without virus protection and risk catastrophe, or you could hand your money to lowlife antivirus companies that treat their customers with contempt. To this day, Microsoft still doesn't bundle virus protection into Windows. But they at least now offer a freely downloadable "Microsoft Security Essentials" tool that eliminates the need to buy third party virus protection. Unfortunately, as we're about to see, even the best antivirus scanning solution isn't really the optimal way to eliminate the risk posed by viruses. As with Apple's iPad, your Nexus 10 uses a different and superior approach.

The App Store Approach to Eliminating Viruses

On a PC, a well-designed antivirus scanner with regularly-updated virus definitions database should eliminate any legitimate worries you have about catching a virus. But there's always a theoretical risk. If a brand new virus should end up on your computer before your antivirus supplier adds it to its database, life could get awful. That's because computer viruses are like AIDS—fairly easy to prevent but extraordinarily difficult to completely remove once an infection has occurred.

Even if you've got a great antivirus scanner that does its job perfectly, there's still overhead attached to this approach to dealing with viruses. Your antivirus software will regularly be downloading and installing new virus definitions from the Internet. Your computer will also slow down every time your virus scanner checks every byte of code in a newly-installed app before allowing it to open.

There's a better and more elegant way to prevent viruses. Apple was the first major company to bring this new approach to market, when it decided to forbid apps from running in iOS unless they were downloaded through Apple's app store. This approach costs iOS users some freedom—unlike Mac and Windows users, iOS users can't download a cool piece of software from a random place on the web and install it. But in giving up this freedom, iOS users gain something of immense value: essentially absolute protection from viruses and malicious code.

That's because, before accepting an app into the iOS app store, Apple will review the code and make sure it's free of viruses and other harmful exploits. Bear in mind that Apple's not reviewing a given piece of software for quality—they're just checking to ensure no viruses or malicious code are present before they publish it to the app store.

As a result of this approach, there's no need for iOS users to ever deal with antivirus software. The app store approach isn't perfect, of course. It means that app developers lose the ability to create whatever they want for the iPhone or iPad—since nothing gets accepted into the app store without Apple's approval. But all in all, the app store approach has turned out to be very popular. That's only to be expected, since the Wild West approach of virus scanners run by shady companies wasn't working out well for anybody but the antivirus companies.

All of this brings us to Google and your Nexus 10. When Google was designing Android, they decided to follow Apple's lead and build an app store of their own. As a result, just like the iPad before it, your Nexus 10 is essentially immune to the threat of viruses. You'll never need a virus scanner, since Google's app store eliminates all risk of viruses.

Google's app store (which is called the Play Store) isn't yet half as impressive as Apple's iOS App Store, since iOS has a big head start in terms of both the number and quality of apps. But already, the Play Store has superb versions of many of the most popular apps on iOS. Over time, there's good reason to expect that Google will make its Play Store experience every bit as slick and customer-friendly as Apple's. It's already darned good, and like everything else in the Android ecosystem it's rapidly improving.

Google's Slate of Free Services

One of the drawbacks to app stores is that they give the platform owner an immense amount of power, and a commensurate temptation to do the wrong thing.

Although neither company will come out and say it, the fact that Apple and Google are competing in several key areas has unleashed a great deal of animosity between the two companies. Google, of course, would love unfettered access when it comes to offering the full range of its services to iPhone and iPad users. Apple, by contrast, as the gatekeeper to the iOS app store, has absolute power to limit Google's access to these devices.

The app store model gives Apple a great deal of power, which the company has consistently used to further its business interests. Apple has repeatedly forced developers to remove key features in order for their apps to be allowed into the store. There's no room for discussion; it's entirely up to Apple to decide what is allowed in its store.

What this means is that some of Google's key services aren't available on the iPad, and Google has no control over which of its services Apple will allow. The bottom line: Google's got the finest suite of free services on the Internet, but if you want unfettered access to them on a tablet, you're going to need to be running Android, not iOS. And since your Nexus 10 runs the very latest version of Android (and likely will for years to come), all of Google's apps and services are available on this platform in their most polished form.

In the next three chapters, we'll look at the core of Google's free services: Gmail, Google Drive, and Google Apps.

Chapter 4

Getting to Know and Love Gmail

While you can use Chrome to access any web-based email (webmail) service, you'll have a much better experience if you use one of the two email apps that came with your Nexus 10. The Gmail app is specifically intended for Gmail users and people with Google Apps-powered custom domains. The other app is simply called "email" and offers generic services that can be configured to work with just about any webmail provider.

Gmail is the best webmail service out there, and your Nexus 10 is set up to take full advantage of Gmail's vast feature set. So if you're currently using email from Yahoo, AOL, Hotmail or another provider, you should strongly consider using the purchase of your Nexus 10 as the motivation to jump ship to Gmail.

You can make a case that Gmail is one of the five or ten most impressive things a consumer-oriented computing company has ever done. Let's take a look at what makes Gmail so great.

Gmail was late to the free webmail party. Both Microsoft and Yahoo had decent webmail for years before Google entered the market with Gmail. But when Gmail launched in 2006, it was immediately better than the competition in many key respects, and the gap has only widened. In June of 2012, Gmail finally beat Microsoft's Hotmail service to become the world's largest provider of free email. I'm surprised it took so long, because Gmail is hands down the best free email service going. There's just no comparison.

What's so great about Gmail? For starters, the service has done a better job of solving the spam problem than any other free webmail offering. I've used Gmail for years, and in a typical month a single piece of spam might penetrate my inbox. By contrast, my experiences with Hotmail and Yahoo Mail have been disastrous. Not only would these services allow far more spam to get through, but they would also falsely mark legitimate emails as spam and put them directly into my spam folder—where they'd go unread.

Gmail, by contrast, gets everything right. Their spam identification algorithm beats anything offered by the competition. Reliable spam detection is the single-most important service an email provider can offer. After all, it's hard enough to keep up with the legitimate emails that demand your attention—who has time to wade through spam?

In addition to having solved the spam problem, Gmail's web interface is super slick and is packed with useful features. There's a great address book built right into Gmail that lets you keep details on all your contacts. Gmail also allows you to shuffle your emails into various folders, so you can, for instance, store every piece of correspondence related to an upcoming wedding in the "Weddings" folder you've created.

You can even set up filters to automatically sort your incoming emails. Those daily emails from your favorite travel deals website could be routed to your "Travel" folder, while emails from a recipe-of-the-day site might go into your "Recipes" folder. Now you can check those emails anytime you want, but they'll never again clutter your primary inbox.

Filters can also be the ultimate way to deal with that weirdo who sends you photos of kittens every week, and who won't take you off his list. You can set up a Gmail filter to delete all future emails the moment they're received from that sender—they'll be vaporized before they reach your inbox!

If all this wasn't enough, Gmail's got one more killer feature: it incorporates Google's industry-leading search technology right into your inbox. You won't believe how useful this will turn out to be.

If you use email often enough, you'll find there are times when you need to quickly find some correspondence from months or years ago. Say, for instance, you had a one-time email exchange with your aunt Erma several years ago. As long as this happened through your Gmail address, you can just type "Erma" into Gmail's searchbox and the email should come right up.

You can make any sort of search refinements you need to quickly find the email you want. For instance, simply by typing your correspondent's email address into the search box, you can instantly obtain every single exchange you've ever had with that person through your Gmail account.

Sometimes, the email you're seeking will be about a topic that has a unique word associated with it. If you know your friend Larry emailed you some details about the Veggie Grill restaurant in West Hollywood, a Gmail search for Veggie Grill should bring that conversation right up. Surrounding Veggie Grill with quotation marks will exclude irrelevant emails that happened to contain both the words Veggie and Grill.

And finally, you can sort your emails by date. If you know you emailed your accountant Jodi in early 2012 about some travel expenses, you could limit your search to the first half of 2012 and include Jodi as a search term. If that still brings up too many emails you could add additional search words like "tax" or "travel" or "deduction" to narrow the results down to the email you are seeking.

This chapter is simply a basic introduction to get you acquainted with Gmail's key features. For a thorough discussion on how to use Gmail as effectively as possible, please turn to Chapter 14.

Now that we've covered Gmail, let's take a look at Google Drive and its built-in suite of productivity apps.

Chapter 5

Google Drive

One of the things Google gives you when you get a Gmail account is your own personal slice of the cloud. The company gives you 5 gigabytes of storage for free. You can bump your storage quota up fivefold for $30 a year, and there's plenty more storage where that came from if you need it. You could store up to 200 gigabytes for only $10 per month, a trivial price to pay if you require off-site and professionally administered backups of key data.

On either Macs or Windows PCs, you can download the Google Drive system extension. Once it's installed, your PC will treat your Google Drive just like it's a USB drive you've physically added to your computer. You'll even see a clickable Google Drive icon in your computer's file manager window. So if you open a couple file manager windows you can start moving or copying any files you wish from your local hard disk to your Google drive. Just be conscious about whether you want to *move* the files, so they exist only on your Google Drive, or whether you wish to *copy* them, so they'll be backed up on your main computer. And if you're keeping the same set of files both locally and on the cloud, be sure you aren't arbitrary about which set you edit. You never want to have any doubt about where the most current versions of your files exist, because the moment you start editing the wrong file you've doomed yourself to losing huge amounts of work.

I have a rule that my latest files are always kept on the cloud, and that's where I edit them. But I make a point of also regularly copying these files to my hard drive for backup. I never, ever edit files that are on my hard drive because the latest version of everything is kept on the cloud. You don't need to do things my way, but you do need to make a rule about where your current files are always kept so you never unwittingly work on outdated files.

When dragging files on a Mac to or from your Google Drive, the default action under Mountain Lion is to move rather than copy. So your files will disappear from your local drive once they're dragged to the cloud. If you want your files to remain on your hard drive after they're copied to the cloud, hold down the option key while dragging and dropping the files. On Windows machines, be sure to use the RIGHT mouse button when picking up and dragging files to your Google Drive. Doing this will bring up a pop-up dialog box before the files are transferred, asking whether the files are to be moved or copied.

If you've been using Google Docs for a while, you may have let a great many documents accumulate over time. They'll all be sitting in chronological order in your Google Drive the first time you open it in your desktop. If you've got a lot of pent-up file clutter, you might as well do some housecleaning. Add some new folders to your Google Drive—just like you would if you were directly accessing your computer's hard drive—and organize your collection of files by dragging them into the appropriate folders.

Anytime you're logged in to your Gmail account, you have access to the files on your Google Drive. So wherever you go, all of your key files will be at hand. In Chrome, Google Drive is currently accessible within Gmail by selecting the *More* menu, and then choosing the *Google Docs*. That's a remnant of the fact that Google Docs predates Google Drive by several years; I expect that Google will soon change that menu item's name from Google Docs to Google Drive.

In any case, accessing Google Drive through a smart phone or tablet's web browser is cramped and unpleasant. You're much better off using the Drive app that came preinstalled on your Nexus 10.

Google Drive is still so new that most Android apps can't yet access it. For instance, the most popular third-party word processor on Android is James McMinn's wonderful free Writer app. In its present form, any documents you create with that app are saved locally to your Nexus 10. That's pretty much the same story for any other document creation app available for Android.

As Google Drive matures and developers get more comfortable with it, I expect it to become widely used by Android apps. But for now, the Nexus 10 isn't much of a nexus at all when it comes to making full use of Google Drive. For the moment, your Nexus 10 gives you a tiny window into a key Google service that's only available in mature form on the desktop.

Chapter 6

Google Docs

Google Docs is an amazing free software offering, and it has undermined and irreparably damaged the business model of Microsoft Office, one of Microsoft's two cash cows. It's probable that Google Docs has been responsible for cutting at least ten billion dollars of value out of Microsoft's market capitalization. (Microsoft's other cash cow is Windows, a product Google has also catastrophically harmed by developing Android.)

Let me now offer a very brief history of office-based software, so you can appreciate how Google came along with its Docs product and disrupted Microsoft's entire business model.

To understand what happened, we need to start all the way back in the early 1980s, with the release of the IBM PC. Pathetically underpowered by today's standards, businesses bought tens of millions of these computers primarily to take advantage of two types of software: word processors and spreadsheets. An employee armed with WordStar and Lotus 1-2-3 was incredibly more productive than one using a traditional Selectric typewriter and an accountant's calculator. With that in mind, businesses didn't mind paying a premium price for this software. Wordstar, the leading PC word processor of the early 1980s, listed for $495. And the Lotus 1-2-3 spreadsheet would set you back $595.

As this niche attracted increasing competition, prices for office software dropped while quality improved. Both WordStar and Lotus managed to blow their early leads. During the 1990s, thanks to its relentless focus, Microsoft's word processing and spreadsheet offerings (Word and Excel) won the war—for a while.

For more than a decade, Microsoft has bundled Word and Excel together along its tragically misused presentation software (Power-Point). Not so long ago, Microsoft Office listed near $500. That's obviously a far greater value than what WordStar or Lotus 1-2-3 offered back in the day, but it still can't compete with free—which is what Google brought to the table when it released Google Docs in 2007.

Thanks to the competition brought by Google, Microsoft Office now sells for under $150, but fewer and fewer people are interested since they can now get most of what they need from Google Docs for free.

Is Google Docs the equal of Microsoft Office? Absolutely not. Microsoft Word, to anyone who's ever had the displeasure of using it, is stuffed with hundreds of features—so many features that at times figuring out basic functionality can be excruciating. By contrast, the word processing component of Google Docs offers a comparatively barebones feature-set. But for most people, who really only need a word processor for correspondence and school or business reports, there's nothing needed that Google Docs can't provide.

Google Docs' spreadsheet component is likewise a pale shadow of Excel's. But once again, Google's spreadsheet has all the basics. If you want to track and total your work expenses or car mileage, for instance, it's more than sufficient. You could also instantly generate a pie chart or bar graph to illustrate your business' earnings or to break down your household expenses by category. Once again, Google Docs doesn't even try to compete with the incredible depth of Microsoft Excel. But 99 percent of spreadsheet users just need the most basic functionality. And if you're amongst that group, Google Docs gives you everything you need in a simple and uncluttered app.

In addition to offering free alternatives to Microsoft Word and

Excel, Google Docs also a offers a Presentation app and a vector-based Drawing app, but these apps are currently only accessible on the desktop through your web browser.

None of these tools come close to matching the feature set of Microsoft Office and similar commercial offerings. But if your needs are basic, Google Docs will more than meet them.

Perhaps the single best thing about Google Docs is the way it stores your files. While Microsoft's Office suite was designed to store your files locally on your hard drive, in Google's suite your files are on your Google Drive. Not only does this cloud storage protect your data from loss, it also makes sharing between computers simpler than ever.

Let's step back a few years so we can better understand cloud computing's advantages in this respect. Plenty of people might own both a laptop and a desktop, and would have reason to shuffle a document back and forth between computers for editing. Under the old model based on local storage, doing this was terribly inconvenient. You'd always need to keep straight in your head whether the most recent version of your document was on your desktop or laptop, and then if you wanted to edit your document on your other machine, you'd have to copy it to disk or email it to yourself. Needless to say, this approach often leads people to become confused about where the latest version of their document exists. It's safe to say that millions of people have, at one time or another, had the agonizing realization that they've spent hours working on an outdated version of their document. Work would be lost, frenzied comparisons of each document would be carried out, and tears would be shed.

But with the cloud-based approach taken by Google Docs, none of this misery need happen. That's because your document doesn't live separately on your desktop, tablet, or laptop—the latest version is always on the cloud.

Suppose you spent an hour on your Nexus 10 writing a first draft of a Google Docs document. Anytime you wanted, you could walk across the room, get on your laptop, and do some additional updates there. When you return to your Nexus 10, your document will contain all the updates you just made on your laptop.

In Google Docs, you never have to worry about whether you've got the latest version of your document, because there's only one version, and it lives on the cloud.

On top of all the other advantages I've gone into, let me add one more: the cloud means you never have think about transporting your data. You can fly halfway around the world without bringing your laptop or Nexus 10, and so long as you know your Gmail password, all of your Google Apps and Google Drive documents will be available through any web browser.

Just as the cloud makes it easy to access the same document from multiple computers and tablets, it also allows multiple people to collaborate on the same document. And, once again, your file is constantly updated on the cloud—so there are no worries about whether a given contributor is reading and modifying an outdated of the document.

When you share a document with Google Docs, you can give that user permission simply to read the document, or to modify it. If you've ever collaborated on a document with others using Microsoft Word or Excel's "Track Changes" feature, you'll find that things work much the same way. That is, as the owner of a document, you'll be able to go through it and accept or reject each proposed addition, edit, or deletion. And again, as with Microsoft Word, each proposed change to the document is stamped with the name of the person responsible.

Cloud-based collaboration works well with two people, but with a group of three or more you'll wonder how you ever lived without it. Because all documents being collectively worked on live on the cloud instead of on someone's hard drive, the stresses associated with keeping track of who has the latest version of the document are eliminated.

Having spent all this time extolling the virtues of cloud-based document storage, there are certainly some situations when you'll want to export your document to your computer's hard disk. Suppose, for instance, you're dealing with a Philistine who doesn't have a Google Apps account and insists on reviewing your work in Word or Excel. No problem. On a Mac or PC just go to your document in Google Docs and then click the File menu in your Chrome Browser. Next, you can select either *Download as* or *Email as attachment.* Either way, you'll be able to save the file in a variety of formats. If your formatting is complex and the recipient is simply going to read your document without marking it up, you might want to choose the PDF option. The PDF format can be opened on any computing platform, and all fonts and formatting of the original document are exactly preserved.

Constant Upgrades

While Google Docs is already a wonderful fit for most people's document creation needs, it's only going to get better. Google is constantly improving Google Docs in large and small ways—from time to time you'll open Google Docs and get a popup window notifying you of some useful new functionality.

This marks a sharp departure from the box-and-disks approach taken by Microsoft and every other traditional software maker. Under that model, when you purchased a copy of Microsoft Office, what you received was basically as good a version as you were going to get (save for perhaps some patches and bug fixes.)

Microsoft would, of course, be diligently working on newer and better versions of the applications you've purchased. But since Microsoft is in the business of selling software, they aren't about to hand over big-time feature upgrades to existing users for free. The Microsoft model is based on the idea that every few years, they'll release a dramatically upgraded version of their Office suite. Everything comes at once, and if you decide there's a feature you can't live without you've got to buy an all-new version of Office. Microsoft also deliberately breaks compatibility with previous versions of Office so that, say, if you own an advertising firm you are eternally obligated to purchase the very latest version. After all, clients will quickly conclude you're an amateur if you tell them that you can't open their documents because you're using an older version of Word or Excel.

Google's model for upgrading its Docs suite is entirely different. Upgrades are small, frequent, and free rather than massive, infrequent, and costly. That's the advantage of using cloud-based apps; it's the easiest thing in the world for Google to deploy a new feature to tens of millions of users overnight. And it's why, for casual users, there's no longer any need to purchase shrink-wrapped general office software. Google Docs and the cloud have you covered.

The Virtues of Native Office Apps

With all the well-deserved praise I've heaped on the collection of Google Docs web apps, I feel obligated to end this chapter by saying a few words in defense of native app alternatives. I don't want to give the impression that cloud-based productivity apps are the perfect tool for everybody in every situation.

You're probably not a professional writer, and you probably don't have heavy-duty spreadsheet needs. So you'll likely be very happy using Google Docs exclusively for your document creation and editing needs. But for people who spend all day writing, or who require complex text formatting, Google Docs' word processor can feel too lightweight for professional use.

I personally use Google Docs all the time for my simple needs. Its word processor is great for short documents, or anything I need to collaborate with others on. And since my spreadsheet needs are likewise very basic, Google Docs has everything I need. I use Google Docs' spreadsheet to record my car mileage and business expenses for my annual tax return.

But for my daily writing sessions, Google Docs isn't good enough, and perhaps never will be. I personally rely on my third generation iPad, and use the IA Writer app—a barebones text editor that has gorgeous typography. Once I've finished a piece, I use Dropbox (available from Dropbox.com) to send it to my Mac. And from there, I typically edit and format my work in Apple's Pages word processor. In the rare instances when I need the highest-quality text formatting, as was the case with the paperback edition of this book, I typeset my drafts in MacTeX.

Professional writers will likely find that IA Writer combined with Pages for the Mac is a more elegant writing environment than anything Android or Google Docs can currently deliver. But this will change. Already, James McMinn's free Writer app (available from the Play Store) provides much of what IA Writer does. For now, though, there's nothing on Android that equals the offerings of Apple's iOS and Mac OS platforms. Until an Android app comes along that compares favorably to IA Writer, I'll stick with my iPad as the place where I compose first drafts.

Your Nexus 10 may not yet offer the ideal writing environment, but for the casual user it's already more than adequate. In fact, you may well decide that when it comes to writing first drafts your Nexus tablet, coupled with a keyboard and the Writer app, provides a nicer experience than that provided by your desktop or laptop.

Chapter 7

Securing Your Data

Anytime you upload your private information to the Internet, you ought to consider the security practices of the people storing your data. Happily, Google employs some of the best security experts on the Internet. That's more than you say for most companies.

You've undoubtedly read stories of major security breaches involving the theft of personal data. In 2011, customer data and credit card numbers were stolen from about 200,000 Citibank customers. In 2012, virtually all personal data on file at social networking site LinkedIn was stolen, with 6.5 million passwords compromised.

These situations revealed stunning incompetence on the part of Citibank and LinkedIn's security team, but sadly there are countless more examples of large breaches enabled through inadequate security practices.

Google's track record regarding security has consistently been excellent. They have a history of not cutting corners when it comes to security, so any data you upload to Google Drive is about as safe as it's likely to be.

Computer criminals know that Google has a strong reputation when it comes to security. As far as these criminals are concerned, it doesn't make sense to devote resources to attempting to break into Google's fortress when other companies, comparatively speaking, have left their front doors wide open.

That said, there's no such thing as a completely secure server. And the enormous trove of personal data held by Google's servers surely represents an inviting target to cyber-criminals, regardless of how formidable Google's security protections may be.

So, should you trust Gmail and Google Drive with your most confidential data? It partly depends on just how confidential and important that information is. A widespread data breach at Google is probably unlikely, but that won't help you if you've stored extraordinarily sensitive information there that somehow gets compromised. You should also know that law enforcement could subpoena Google at any time, if it can convince a judge that you've likely stored incriminating files.

Here are the things you might think twice about uploading to the cloud: password lists; bank and financial institution account information; and any file that might expose you to prosecution, litigation, or public embarrassment.

There's a simple precaution you can use to make the data on your Google drive vastly more secure: choose a robust password, greater than 8 characters, that contains lowercase and uppercase letters as well as numbers. Also, you never, ever want to re-use your password for other services. Suppose, for instance, you use the same email address and password for both Google and Netflix. If Netflix were to get hacked, the thieves could gain everything they need to access your Google account!

But if Google ever falls victim to a major security breach, or receives a subpoena, even a well-chosen password won't protect you. That's why it's smart to never upload any highly sensitive data to Google without encrypting it first. That way, even if Google's servers suffer a major breach, the intruder would still have to get past your encryption to access your data—and given how much unencrypted data the thieves would likely have stolen, it's unlikely they'd devote the significant resources required to cracking one user's encryption. If you want to use encryption, you're best off using your Mac or PC to encrypt your data, as these platforms have free and mature encryption tools. There are free Mac and PC versions of PGP (the most popular encryption standard) available at GnuPG.com.

If you want to encrypt your data with your Nexus 10, AGP is probably the best bet. It's not nearly as mature as GnuPG, but I expect there to be rapid advances in the quality of encryption software for Android in the not-too-distant future.

Personally, though, I'd never upload my most sensitive data to the cloud—even if I encrypted it. Instead, I prefer to save it to a USB thumb drive—ideally in encrypted form. These days, you can buy a USB thumb drive from Amazon.com for about $10. But know that your Nexus 10 can't currently save through its USB port unless you've rooted the operating system. I therefore handle all my passwords and the storage of sensitive information on my Macintosh.

I think the safest way to handle confidential information is to save your most sensitive files to a USB thumb drive, and then hide the drive somewhere in your house. You'll gain a big measure of safety from burglars and remote hackers alike if these files are not stored anywhere on your computer. Note that smart burglars will check bedrooms and computer rooms first, so hide your drive elsewhere. Given how tiny USB drives are, and the fact that a typical burglar spends less than twelve minutes in a house, you should be able to find a spot that will make your thumb drive all but impossible to find. Alternately, you could rent a safety deposit box at your local bank. For an added measure of security, you can encrypt your files before copying them to your thumb drive—so even if your drive falls into the wrong hands your data will still be extremely difficult to access.

Finally, no matter where you store your sensitive data, remember that all your security efforts mean nothing if you leave unencrypted versions of your sensitive data laying about. Give some thought to how easy it would be for a thief who stole your Nexus 10 to access your important confidential data. Then come up with a plan that puts this key information out of easy reach.

Chapter 8

The Home Screen

At the heart of your Nexus 10 is the user interface that allows you to navigate your device. As with an iPad, most of your Nexus 10's navigation is based on the Home screen.

You may wish to skip this chapter and instead watch some of the videos I've created that cover this subject. Using and modifying the Home screen is really simple, but it's probably easier understood by video than by text. Just visit NexusGuides.com to access my free instruction videos.

Your Home screen is totally customizable. And while the Nexus 10's navigation features are a bit harder to figure out than the comparable interface on an iPad, Android navigation is also (as we're about to see) a lot more flexible and powerful than what Apple's iOS offers. This chapter will show you how to personalize your Home screen to best suit your needs.

It's worthwhile to invest some time playing with and modifying your Home screen, since the more you personalize it to your needs, the more useful your Nexus 10 will be to you. An hour spent modifying your Home screen and wrapping your head around its interface will go a long way toward allowing you to get the most out of your Nexus 10. If you've done a good job of organizing your Home screen, you'll always be just a step away from pretty much anything you could want to do.

The Home screen has three components: the Navigation Bar, the Dock, and the apps/widgets section. The Navigation Bar and the Dock that sits atop it take up the bottom inch of your screen. The remainder of your Home screen is devoted to apps and widgets. Let's now go through how to use the Navigation Bar, the Dock, and the apps/widgets section.

The Navigation Bar

The Navigation Bar is located at the very bottom of every screen you access. This black bar is always present wherever you go, except for the times that an app goes into full-screen mode (such as when playing a game or a Netflix movie.) The Navigation bar features three items:

1. On the left: the Back button. Each time you touch the Back button, you will page back to the previous screen. Note that different apps treat the Back button differently, so this button won't always behave the way you expect.

2. In the center: the Home button. Disregard for a moment the fact that this button looks more like an opened business envelope than a house. Anytime you touch the Home button, you're just one step away from 95 percent of the things you're likely to want to do.

3. On the right: an opened-apps button. This lets you see the apps you've recently had open, and that are still in memory. I don't like this button's implementation at all, and I think it'll confuse most users. But go ahead and touch it to check it out. I expect that most people will rarely use it.

The Dock

The next item above the Navigation Bar on your Home screen is the Dock. The dock has room for six apps or folders. You can remove or modify everything in the dock except for the Apps screen icon, which is always in the center of your Dock and shows six squares in a circle.

Touching the Apps screen icon takes you to a screen showing, in alphabetical order, the first forty apps installed on your Nexus 10. On this Apps screen, you can swipe left (rub your finger from right to left across the screen) to access secondary Apps screens.

After you've swiped through however many Apps screens you have, swiping left one more time will bring up the Widgets screens.

What we want to do is to set up your Nexus 10 so that you need to access the Apps screen as rarely as possible. And the way we accomplish that is to give some thought to the apps you most frequently use. These apps should be moved to your Dock. Once they're in your Dock, they can be accessed directly from the Home screen.

If you've ever used an iPad or a recent Mac or Windows PC, you should be instantly at home with the Nexus 10's Dock. On iPads and Macs, Apple calls this area the Dock. And on PCs, Microsoft calls it the Taskbar. Whatever they're called, their default position is along the bottom of your screen. On the Nexus 10, as I mentioned, the Dock only appears on the Home screens, just above the Navigation bar.

The Nexus 10's Dock works much the same as the Docks you've used on other platforms. The point of a Dock is to hold your most commonly-used apps, so that they can be accessed from your Home screens at a moment's notice. And since the Dock contains the same stuff no matter which Home screen you're on, you'll always be just one or two touches away from all of your favorite apps.

Chances are you will ultimately have more than a dozen apps you use frequently. But your Nexus 10 Dock has just eight available slots (the ninth slot is, as previously mentioned, reserved for the center icon that brings up the Apps screen.) So what do you do if you've got twenty or thirty apps you want kept in your Dock? Well, the Nexus 10 Dock has a great feature that is not yet on Macs or iPads. That is, the Dock supports folders.

Let's say that your favorite games are Angry Birds, AlphaWave, and RipTide GP. You've already purchased these games. Now you want to create a Games folder in your Dock that provides access to these games. How do you do that? It's easy:

1. Touch the Home button in the Navigation Bar and then touch the Apps screen button in the Dock.

2. Find and touch the Angry Birds icon and hold your finger on it for a second. The screen will change from the Apps screen to the Home screen, while the icon remains beneath your finger. Don't remove your finger from the Angry Birds icon. Now, drag the icon into a vacant slot in your Dock and remove your finer.

3. With Angry Birds now in your Dock, touch on the Apps screen button again. Touch and hold your finger on the Alphawave icon, and when the Home screen comes up, drag Alphawave on top of your Angry Birds icon. Repeat this step to drag the RipTide GP icon onto your Angry Birds icon.

4. You'll notice that once you drag a file onto another file in the Dock, the icon changes to a circle showing the enclosed App icons. The circle indicates that the slot in your Dock is occupied by a folder of apps rather than a single app. When you touch this folder, it'll bring up a small popup window showing the enclosed apps. You can then of course touch the desired app to launch it, but let's get a bit fancy first. If you've followed my example so far, you'll have three games in your popup window. At the bottom of this popup window it'll say, "Unnamed Folder". Well, let's give it a name. Just touch the "Unnamed Folder" text and it'll disappear and be replaced by a cursor. In this case, you can type in "Games". Boom, now you've got a

Games folder in your Dock, and you can drag new games into it anytime you want.

So now that we've learned how to add files and folders to the Dock, let me finish this coverage by making a couple of additional points. You ought to think about which categories of apps you will spend most of your time using. If you're a serious musician, and expect to frequently use audio production and virtual instrument apps to create music, it would make sense to group these various apps into a folder named Music. If you like to draw, you might create a Drawing folder for the various art apps you purchase. You get the idea. You've got eight modifiable slots in your Dock, each able to hold a custom folder based on the categories of apps you most frequently use.

Alternately, you could create a secondary Home screen specifically for your core interest—and fill that Home screen with the apps and widgets that cater to that interest. Just swipe left on your Home screen and it'll bring up an empty secondary Home screen for you to set up. You can repeat this process to set up as many secondary Home screens as you like. Most people won't need any secondary Home screens because they'll be able to fit everything they need onto a single screen. That said, a secondary Home screen could be extremely valuable. You could, for instance, create one that's devoted to the apps used by your business—leaving your main Home screen devoted solely to apps for personal use. Or you could have a secondary Home screen filled with your favorite games.

The other thing you might want to keep in mind is that while you can add a ton of apps to a given folder in your Dock, every app you add makes the navigation a bit more cumbersome. So if you spend 95 percent of your gaming time playing four games, but have thirty games on your Nexus 10, you might want to only include your top four games in your Games folder, so that they can be accessed in a heartbeat. You can always visit the apps screen to open a game you rarely play.

The Apps/Widgets Section

The Navigation Bar and Dock only covers the bottom inch of your Home screen(s). The remainder of these screens are reserved for apps and widgets.

When first Nexus tablet arrived, I found the default Home Screen setup to be ugly and baffling. All of the area on the Home screen was devoted to widgets of items from the Google Play library. When I think of libraries, I think of an elegant wood-paneled reading room at a university library. When I think of the way the library looked on my Home screen, I think of an episode of Hoarders.

I didn't realize that all this dreck monopolizing my Home screen was just a bunch of widgets that could be easily deleted and replaced with apps and widgets that I selected according to my needs.

It's easy to customize your Home screen. First, you need to clear space by resizing or eliminating the Widgets already on your Home screen. To do this, just touch a widget until it's selected. Next, either resize it by dragging and moving an edge, or delete the widget entirely by grabbing its center and dragging and dropping the widget onto the "x Delete" field atop the screen.

Now that you've cleared out some space, you want to choose the most useful apps or widgets you've got, and move them onto the Home screen.

I discussed moving apps to the Dock in the previous section. Moving apps to the Home screen works exactly the same way, except you drop them into the apps/widgets section of your Home screen rather than into the Dock. To recap what I wrote earlier, just touch the apps button at the center of the Navigation Bar, hold your finger down on the desired app, and drag it to whichever position you'd like on the apps/widgets portion of your home screen. Just like I mentioned in my coverage of moving apps into the Dock, you can create folders in your Home Page's apps/widgets section by dropping one app atop another. Once on your Home screen you can drag your app to the right to drop it onto secondary Home screens.

While you can't drop widgets into your Dock, you can drop them into the apps/widgets section of the Home screen. Doing this works much the same way as adding apps to this area. That is, you touch the Apps button in the navigation bar, and swipe left until you reach the widget screens. Then you simply hold your finger on whichever widget you'd like to install. Your Home screen will come up, and you then drag the widget to the desired location—dragging right if you wish to access secondary Home screens.

Many widgets can be resized. To resize a widget on your Home screen just hold your finger on it until it's selected. If it's resizable, you'll see a blue dot at the midpoint of each side. Press your finger on one of the dots and drag it to shrink or expand the widget as desired.

Finding New Widgets

As you'll discover as you page through the widget section in your Apps pages, Android includes a bunch of incredibly useful widgets. But you're not limited to using only these.

For instance, I wanted to add a stocks ticker widget to my Home screen. There are unfortunately no stock widgets bundled into Android, so I went to the Play Store and searched for "stock widget." I found a great widget called, "Android Stocks Tape Widget." This widget gives me a live ticker on my Home screen showing constant updates of my entire investment portfolio.

Android's collection of third-party widgets is growing constantly. There are alternate versions of widgets that are bundled with your Nexus 10, along with a variety of widgets that show custom information. Just go to the Play store, touch the search (magnifying glass) button, and search for "widget." You'll find dozens of great widgets that can extend the usefulness of your Home screens.

Chapter 9

Essential Apps

Just as it's worthwhile to spend an hour or so playing with widgets and setting up your Home screen exactly to your liking, it's likewise a good idea to spend some time browsing Google's Play Store. Much of the value you get from your Nexus 10 will come from custom apps downloaded from this store. The Play Store features thousands of apps, from categories that include games, productivity, image editing, money management, music, and many more.

Apple's App Store is still more attractive and better designed than the Google Play Store. And, more importantly, iOS still has vastly more apps to choose from than does Android. But Android app producers are rapidly closing the gap. Many of the marquee apps on iOS are now available as Android versions.

So let's now run through some of the main categories of apps available from Google's Play Store. I hope that this chapter will turn you on to some new ideas that will enable you to get more out of your Nexus 10 than you thought possible.

This chapter begins with several key apps that ship with your Nexus 10, and then we'll move on to cover a number of other apps that are worth downloading through the Play Store.

Default Apps that Ship with Your Nexus 10

Settings

You'll probably use the Settings app frequently since it lets you do so many things. I use it often enough that it's got a place in my Dock. I'll describe this app's most important features here.

You can use the Settings app to turn on or off Bluetooth or Wi-Fi. You can always get an extra hour or so of battery life by turning off Wi-Fi—a nice thing to know if you're traveling and don't have easy access to power outlets.

If you turn on Bluetooth and then touch the *Bluetooth* item in the settings menu, you'll be taken through the steps to pair your device to any nearby Bluetooth-equipped keyboards, speakers, or headsets that are turned on.

It's a good idea to check the *Storage* entry occasionally to see how close you are to filling up your Nexus 10's memory. You'll see a chart showing how much memory is currently occupied by apps, photos, music, video, and downloads. The final line will show you how much local storage space remains. If things are getting tight, you can delete apps and locally stored files to free up space.

Unlike the iPad, the Nexus 10 doesn't display on its Home screen the percentage of battery power remaining. To know precisely how much juice you've got left you need to go into settings and touch the battery icon.

The Google Play Store

In Android there's an app for every purpose, including one that lets you go shopping for other apps. Use the Play Store app to browse for apps, music, eBooks, magazines, or video. While iOS's ecosystem has an App Store for app purchases and iTunes for digital media purchases, in Android everything you buy is through the Play Store.

Using the Play Store, you shouldn't have any trouble finding what you're seeking. Android's apps offerings are, these days, probably growing nearly as fast as iOS's collection.

Calendar

Your Nexus 10 comes bundled with Google's Calendar app. By touching the + button in the upper-right corner of this app, a screen will come up that allows you to enter upcoming events. For events that either last all day, or simply have to be done at some undesignated point on a given day, touch the "All Day" checkbox in the event entry screen.

If you sign into Gmail through your desktop or laptop, you can access your calendar through the black menu bar atop your web browser's window. When using Google Calendar through a Mac or PC, you'll gain many configuration options that are unavailable on your Nexus 10. The most important of these is the ability to create secondary calendars. You could, for instance, have a "Home" calendar and a "Work" calendar. With these in place you could conveniently scan to all your "Work" tasks over the next week, then toggle off "Work" and toggle on "Home" to see your home and family commitments.

What's more, you can grant others access to specific calendars. Just hover your mouse pointer over a given calendar's name, click the down arrow, and select *Share this Calendar.* You might give a coworker access to seeing your Work calendar (while the Home calendar stays private), and simultaneously give your spouse access to your Home calendar.

One last thing about calendars: I think Google's calendar system is so good that it deserves to run your life. If your current calendaring is based on Apple's iCloud you may want to think about exporting the contents of your calendar to Google Calendar. Here's how you do it:

1. In Apple's Calendar app on a desktop or laptop, choose *File > Export > Export.*

2. From Google Calendar on a desktop or laptop, Choose *Other Calendars* and import the file you just saved.

3. Finally, connect the Calendar apps on your Mac and/or iOS device to your new Google-hosted calendar. On the Mac, open the Calendar app and select *File > Preferences.* Click on the + button. In the window that opens choose Google as your account type and then type your Gmail address and password. On the iPhone or iPad, open the Settings app and choose *Mail, Contacts, Calendars.* Add your Gmail account. Next, switch off Calendars under the iCloud entry and switch on Calendars under the Gmail entry.

Congratulations: your iOS devices, Macintosh, and Nexus tablet now share the same calendar. Now, when you add or change a date, it's synchronized over the cloud to all your computers, smart phones, and tablets. Note that with default calendar settings, it can take up to fifteen minutes for a new or changed Google Calendar entry to become visible on your Mac or iPad.

Contacts (People App)

Whenever I get a business card, or receive somebody's full contact info by email I make sure to take a moment to enter it into Google's Contacts section. I prefer to do this at my Mac because the added screen real estate makes this data entry a lot more convenient. The pathway into Google's Contacts list in Gmail is currently well hidden: you need to click the Mail button and then select Contacts from the popup window.

You could also update your Google Contacts using your Nexus 10's built-in People app (why they named this app People rather than Contacts is a mystery for the ages).

Regardless of which device you use to create a contact, that information will be available everywhere you use Gmail. So, when using Gmail on my Nexus 10, all I have to do is type "Steven" into the "To" header of my email, and the twelve different Stevens in my contact list come up in a pop up menu. I just select the Steven I want and I'm in business.

Alternately, I could have typed "Perkins" and my friend Steven Perkins would have come up as the only option, as he's the only Perkins in my Google contact list.

Downloads

This is an essential app with minimal functionality. You'll use the Downloads app to open or access a file (audio, PDF, whatever) that you've downloaded from Chrome or Gmail. Once you've opened the Downloads app, you'll be able to open your file, share it, or delete it.

Navigation

You can use your Nexus 10 as a GPS system for your car, although it's a little too big for the task. I'd rather use a Nexus 7 or a dedicated GPS device.

The Navigation app pre-installed on your Nexus 10 has a number of limitations. To use it, you must begin with a Wi-Fi connection, so as to download your route and the turn-by-turn navigation from the cloud. Every dedicated GPS navigator will allow you to veer off the specified route, and will respond to these route deviations by generating revised directions to your destination. But not the Nexus 10's default navigation app. Go off course and the unit just lapses into sullen silence as if you've hurt her feelings. You can forget about receiving revised directions.

The Navigation app also gives new meaning to the phrase, "You can't go home again." Because once it's time to head home, you're not going to receive turn-by-turn spoken directions unless you first tap into a Wi-Fi network. That said, you're often halfway familiar with getting home—in which case all you need to do is follow the blue onscreen route tracing back to your home that will be presented on the Nexus 10's screen.

There are alternative navigation apps that overcome the limitations of Google's official app. You may want to download NavFree or CoPilot from the Play Store. Neither app has received consistently glowing reviews, but they're certainly worth keeping an eye on if you're looking for a better navigation experience than what your Nexus 10's default Navigation app offers.

All things taken into consideration, navigation on the Nexus 10 is dreadful yet still worthwhile. I much prefer relying on its spoken directions than to do what I used to do—read printed directions generated by Google Maps. But if I'm ever headed someplace that I know is hard to find, there's comfort in over-preparing: bringing along printed round-trip directions as a back-up, while primarily using the Nexus 10's Navigation app for turn-by-turn spoken directions. Your Nexus 10 will get you there—probably. And if it doesn't you'll have a map and printed driving directions to fall back on.

So whatever its flaws, the Navigation app is well worth using if you need driving directions only occasionally. And I've no doubt that over time, either the default Navigation app or one of its competitors will blossom into a first-rate navigation tool.

Until then, if you're somebody with frequent navigation needs, forget about the Nexus 10 and spend a couple hundred dollars to buy a high-end GPS device. For the rest of us, we've got an imperfect but useful solution for our occasional navigation needs.

Recommended Apps from the Google Play Store

Timers and Alarm Clocks

Whether it's used for cooking, power naps, meditation, or the Pomodoro Technique, a timer app will make your Nexus 10 vastly more valuable. In fact, I probably use my timer more than any other app on my Nexus 10. I recommend Roberto Leinardi's Kitchen Timer, which is good but not great. I've yet to find a timer for Android that is as excellent as Timer+ on iOS.

For an alarm clock, try Alarm Clock Plus from Binary Tactics. The ad-free version costs just 99 cents, and will give you an alarm clock far more capable than any clock radio you could buy.

Note that both of these apps allow you to put your Nexus 10 to sleep to conserve battery power (your Nexus 10 will automatically wake up when it's time to play the alarm). This ability to wake your Nexus 10 is a nice feature for a timer and an essential feature for an alarm clock. Just to be clear, when you turn off your Nexus 10 in the usual way you're actually putting it to sleep. To truly turn your Nexus 10 off, you need to hold down the power button for a second and then touch the *Power off* menu option that will appear on your screen. Generally the only reasons to do this are to reboot Android in order to reset apps that are misbehaving, or to prepare your Nexus 10 to be stored away unused for a few days or longer.

The Kindle App

The built-in Play Books app can read eBooks purchased from the Google Play store. You can also download the Kindle app to read eBooks purchased from Amazon.com.

I bought a Kindle a couple years ago and fell in love with it. But I never use it anymore, even though I buy most of my books in the Kindle format.

When the third generation iPad came out, I migrated to it as my primary reading platform. The Kindle was still better in terms of being vastly lighter, and having a non-backlit e-ink display (which is much easier on the eyes.) But the incredible clarity of the iPad's retina display made up for the device's extra weight, so I switched to doing most of my reading on the iPad's Kindle app.

With the release of the Nexus 10, I've migrated once again. The Nexus 10's display is even better and sharper than my iPad's. I'll have no reason to use my iPad once the Nexus 10 gets a top-notch RSS reader and a basic text editor with high quality typography.

Reader Apps

I don't like to surf the web on my Nexus 7 because the screen is too cramped for my taste, and many websites render poorly. But the experience of using Chrome on the Nexus 10 is far better. That said, many websites still aren't optimized for tablets, so you're likely to encounter many sites that don't look so great on your Nexus 10. This shortcoming should be remedied relatively quickly, since all the top websites today are rapidly embracing mobile platforms, and are being developed with responsive frameworks that work great regardless of whether you're using a PC, tablet, or smart phone.

Anyway, when it comes to online reading, in many cases RSS readers and read-it-later applications are a better choice than web browsers. And both of these app categories work marvelously on the Nexus 10. That's because these sorts of apps pull the main content from a given web page, and reformat it for easy viewing. You're not locked into the source website's design in order to view its content—it's been extracted and displayed on the screen as if it were a page from a book. Formatted in this way, the Nexus 10 becomes a wonderful platform for reading your favorite web content.

Let's now look at conventional RSS readers, magazine-style RSS readers, and read-it-later apps.

Conventional RSS Readers

An RSS reader is basically an automated web browser. Many people bookmark their favorite five or ten sites, and manually visit these sites each day. They click one bookmark, read what they want, then click their next bookmark, and repeat this process until they've gone through all their bookmarks. This approach to web browsing entails a surprisingly large amount of needless work—there's a better way.

By using an RSS reader, the task of visiting each of your favorite websites is handled automatically. All you need to do is to tell your RSS reader your favorite sites, and every time you open your reader it'll go and get all the latest articles for you.

What's more, RSS readers pull the text from the website so it can be read in a format optimized for your Nexus 10.

Although it takes a few minutes to set up an RSS reader, the benefits are immense and immediate. Three highly-rated and free RSS readers available from the Google Play store are: gReader, RSSDemon, and Google's own Google Reader.

Magazine-Style RSS Readers

I consider the Flipboard and Pulse News apps to be RSS for dummies (no offense to dummies intended). Both apps offer a familiar magazine-like experience, and you can add your favorite websites to create your own custom magazine that's updated daily.

Both Flipboard and Pulse News feature a pleasant interface and a gorgeous design. Most users will be blissfully unaware that they're really using a prettied-up RSS reader. But that's fine. These are beautifully designed apps that, to borrow from Bill Gates' billion-dollar idea, "embraces and extends" the concept of RSS to make it appeal to the masses.

These apps not only simplify RSS, they go it one better—at least for anyone who believes a picture is worth a thousand words. By auto-extracting photos from the websites you follow, these readers provide a more visually striking experience than what a traditional RSS reader can offer.

I use these apps on occasion, but for my daily RSS reading, I much prefer the traditional readers described in the previous section. But that puts me in the minority—most people prefer a more visually-oriented magazine-style layout to what conventional RSS readers deliver.

Read-it-Later Apps

Sometimes you'll be on your main computer and you'll encounter a lengthy article you want to read. But doing extended reading on a desktop or laptop is unpleasant. Fortunately, with the advent of tablets, a new type of app was invented that gracefully solves this problem. These apps are tablet or smart phone based, and integrate with a "bookmarklet" on your desktop or laptop. Whenever you find a long article while web browsing that you wish to read on your Nexus 10, you can either click the bookmarklet or send the article's URL to a custom email address and the piece will show up in your Nexus 10's read-it-later app.

The original and probably the best of these apps is Instapaper, which was originally released for iOS. The app's developer has since ported a version to Android. I've purchased Instapaper and urge you to buy it as well. At $2.99 it's a great deal for an app that will make your Nexus 10 vastly more useful.

Word Processing and Spreadsheets

Google Drive on the Nexus 10 currently offers only two of the five Google Docs apps that are available on the desktop. Luckily they're the two most important apps: a word processor called "Documents" and a spreadsheet called, well, "Spreadsheet." I guess when you give apps away for free, you need not spend time dreaming up fancy names for them.

On the Nexus 10, the Documents component of Google Drive is useful for basic work. If you're going to write something longer than a paragraph, I would definitely hook up a USB or Bluetooth keyboard. On the Nexus 10, the screen is already undersized for word processing or spreadsheet work, so taking up nearly half that space with a virtual keyboard seems masochistic.

For general word processing, I think you'll be happier working in the cloud-based Google Drive apps on your desktop of laptop. This is doubly true if your document requires substantial formatting. While I wouldn't want to compose lengthy documents or do substantial formatting on my Nexus 10, it's certainly nice to know I can read or edit my documents when I'm away from my desktop computer.

And forget about doing any real spreadsheet work on your Nexus 10. Apart from quickly reviewing or updating key data on a small spreadsheet, I can't imagine spending any time accessing spreadsheets on my Nexus 10. To comfortably use a spreadsheet, you need plenty of screen real estate. Even laptops are too constricted for my taste, and a typical laptop's screen is much bigger than the Nexus 10's screen.

To-Do Lists and Record Keeping

There are a number of to-do list and project management apps in the Play Store. This category has turned into a fetish for me, since everything I do is organized through through the principles laid out in David Allen's book, *Getting Things Done.* I find that to-do lists and project management work is more gracefully handled on the desktop than on a tablet, and I'm a great fan of Apple's Reminders app on the Macintosh.

That said, a simple and minimalist to-do list app can add a great deal of value to your tablet or smart phone. There's a lot of competition in this niche, and many of the Android apps I've looked at are buggy or have a needlessly steep learning curve. I suggest going to the Play Store and downloading the Tasks Free app, which is elegant and very easy to learn. If after trying it out you decide you like it, upgrade to the company's 99 cent Tasks app which is ad-free and offers additional features.

Evernote is the best known personal information manager, and it's got a staggering array of features. It's definitely a worthwhile tool for anyone who needs to keep any sort of records, from tax deductions to web clippings to school notes to recipes. Fans of the iPad view the Evernote app for Android as being vastly superior to the iOS version, so this is a must-download app if you have a lot of personal information you want to store and manage.

Games

There's no way to do the Nexus 10's wealth of games justice in a few paragraphs. So I'll just say that what Pac-Man was to 1980s arcade games, Angry Birds is to tablets. It's of course available on the Nexus 10. Start with the original (avoid the Seasons and Space sequels until you're hooked), since the original is on the easy side of the difficulty spectrum.

The gap between the iOS and Android stores is greatest where games are concerned, but there are already a number of great games available on the Nexus 10. I'm not a huge gamer, and whatever I'd recommend will be soon surpassed by newer games. But in addition to Angry Birds I can recommend Fruit Ninja and Flick Golf as fun and easy ways to pass time.

If you like pinball, Zen Pinball THD is incredible, and it comes with one free table. Additional tables are only a dollar or two apiece.

One annoyance to be aware of for both Android and iOS games: these platforms both allow an odious practice called, "In App Purchases." Many games lean heavily on this pricing model. In some cases, the game is free, but you need to expand your character or weapons system with paid purchases in order to finish the game.

Apple's App Store clearly notes when games have In App Purchases. The Play Store offers no such indication—although you'll often see complaints about In App Purchase requirements in customer reviews. I personally refrain from buying these games, as I'd rather pay a fair price up-front for my games, without getting nickel-and-dimed to death later.

Audio

Much of the value you'll get from your Nexus 10 comes from its outstanding abilities to play audio. You can use the headphone jack to connect your device to your home or car stereo. And if you really want to get fancy, you can get a bluetooth-equipped speaker system and output your music wirelessly. These bluetooth speaker units can be purchased for as little as $30.

Once you've got a decent audio connection, there are all sorts of ways to obtain quality audio programming.

Google would no doubt prefer you to purchase all your audio and video from the Play Store. But you've got other options, especially where music is concerned. Amazon.com has an Amazon MP3 app that lets you stream or download music. Anything you've bought since their "Digital Music Locker" premiered in April 2011 will be available.

There are a number of apps that let you stream radio stations from around the world. I recommend Stitcher, which not only lets you find and listen to countless radio stations, it also provides a good interface for discovering and playing podcasts.

Podcasts are syndicated by RSS the same way blogs are—the only difference is that podcasts typically have an audio file attached along with each entry's text. Stitcher is to conventional podcast players what Flipboard is to RSS readers—it's easier to use and figure out than a conventional player, but not so great if you simply want to subscribe to a feed and have everything downloaded and available in one place. If you get hooked on a podcast and want to never miss a show, you may prefer a traditional podcast player like CPU Guy's "Podcast Player."

The trouble using Stitcher to access radio stations is that you'll listen to tons of commercials, and the music may not match your taste. For many Nexus 10 users the Pandora app is a better choice. You enter a favorite band into Pandora and you'll hear a stream of songs from similar artists. Pandora has fewer commercials than radio, but still too many for my taste (but then, as far as I'm concerned, even one commercial is one commercial too many). Fortunately, for just $36 per year, you can bump up your Pandora service to a commercial-free stream with higher-quality audio.

Alternately, if you'd rather build your own playlist, consider Spotify. They've got an incredible selection of music. Typically when I search for a track on Spotify I find exactly what I'm looking for, plus several alternate tracks I'm equally excited about. I subscribe to Spotify's $5 per month desktop/laptop plan, which lets me listen to unlimited music, commercial free. For $10 per month you get higher quality audio, and the ability to listen on Android and iOS devices. What's more, at the $10 rate, you're allowed to download music to your device so you can listen to it on the road through the Spotify player. Note that with Spotify, you never own any of the music you download—once you cancel your subscription, your access to the music you've downloaded vanishes.

Video

For video rentals and purchases, you're mostly stuck with using the Play Store for now. But by the time you're reading this, Amazon.com may have have released a video app for the Nexus 10. They released a video app for iOS in August of 2012, and I can't imagine Android will be far behind.

Apart from renting videos from the Play Store, the Nexus 10 has three terrific options for streaming video. Android 4.2 ships with a very nice YouTube app, which is well worth exploring. The more often you choose Thumbs Up or Thumbs Down on the videos you watch, the more YouTube will know your taste, and the better it will get at offering recommendations.

Netflix works a lot like YouTube, except it's a paid service full of feature films and television series. There are no commercials, and Netflix's recommendation system is remarkably good, so it's wise to rate most of the videos you watch so that Netflix can make suggestions tailored as closely to your viewing tastes as possible. At just $8 per month for unlimited streaming, I consider Netflix a viable alternative to cable.

Hulu is similar to Netflix but it's more oriented towards network television shows, and its basic version is free. But on Hulu, you're stuck watching commercials, even with their paid service which goes for $8 per month. Still, you won't see nearly as many commercials as you do on network or cable television. And if you're excited by the prospect of watching the entire catalog of old shows like "Hill Street Blues" or "The A Team," Hulu is a dream come true.

Chapter 10

Google Talk

Not to be confused with Google Voice (a service that lets you make free phone calls to telephones), Google Talk lets you exchange text messages with other Google users, as well as participate in voice or video chats. Your Nexus 10 features a front-facing video camera that automatically turns on when you accept or initiate a Google Talk video chat.

If you've ever used Skype (or, for that matter, Apple's Facetime), you'll be right at home with the Google's Talk app the first time you use it. The Talk app is elegantly designed and features a superb user interface.

The app's main screen lists people you've exchanged emails with who have Google accounts. If you look closely, you'll see that this screen is divided into three sections. First, in white, is an alphabetical list of the friends you've recently connected with over Google Talk and who are online. Next, in light gray, you've got another alphabetical list of the friends you haven't connected with recently but who are currently signed in to their Google accounts.

Finally, in dark gray, you'll see yet another alphabetical list of your friends who aren't online. In a nice touch, Google Talk converts the profile photos of these offline friends to black and white.

If you look beneath the names of each person in the first two lists, you'll see either a green dot or an orange dot. A green dot means that they've been interacting with Gmail (or another Google product) within the past fifteen minutes. So if you send these people a text message or a video chat request, they're likely to see it immediately.

People with an orange dot beneath their names are currently logged into Google, but they haven't interacted with their account in more than fifteen minutes. So if you contact them through Google Talk, they may not see your message or chat request. Conceivably, they're not even at their computer. I could log into Gmail and then leave town for the day, and my Google Talk friends would see an orange dot beneath my name for the entire time I was away—as long as I left my computer on.

Alongside each of your Google Talk friends, on the right side of the screen, you may see a microphone or a video camera icon. Touch that icon and you'll send a voice or video chat request to that friend. But if you touch the main entry for your friend (anything to the left of the microphone or video icon), the Talk app will open a window where you can send each other texts.

As you might expect for a company founded as a search engine, Google's got a great search feature built into the Talk app. Suppose, months ago, one of your friends during a text chat gave you some information about Cannondale bicycles, and now you're finally ready to act on that information and to make your purchase. Unfortunately, you can't remember whether your friend advised you to get Cannondale's Synapse Alloy or its Synapse Carbon model. Fortunately, it's easy to find that particular Google Talk exchange in your archives. Just touch the magnifying glass button in Google Talk and do a search for Cannondale, and every Google Talk text message you've ever exchanged that mentioned the company will come up.

What if you want to chat with someone, but you've never connected with that person through his or her Gmail account before? Just touch the + icon in the upper right corner of Google Talk's menu, and you can send a chat request to your friend's email. Note that your friend will need a Google account to chat with you. And when I sent a Google Talk invitation to a Hotmail account for testing purposes, the good people at Microsoft obligingly routed my request to the Junk folder.

Finally, what if this whole world of Google Talk video chatting whets your appetite for more? Using Google Talk, you can only chat with your friends one-on-one. But if you download the Google+ app, you'll be able to participate in live video "hangouts" with up to ten people at a time.

Google+ is a wonderfully powerful and flexible service that's outside the scope of this book. For many reasons, I vastly prefer Google+ to Facebook, and your Nexus 10 comes bundled with an outstanding Google+ app. The book to read to get your feet wet with Google+ is Guy Kawasaki's *What the Plus!: Google+ for the Rest of Us.* It's just 99 cents from the Google Play bookstore or from the Amazon.com Kindle store.

Chapter 11

Voice Search

It's so small anyone could miss it; it's the tiny icon showing a microphone in the upper right corner of your Home screen. And it's got a yawn-inducing name: Google Voice Search. But the first time you push it, you may feel catapulted ten years into the future and that the aliens are about to land.

Even in its early release, it's clear that Google has poured tremendous resources into its Voice Search. In fact, it's obvious that both Google and Apple came to an identical realization many years ago: that one day people would want to interact by voice with an intelligent online assistant. Today, Apple has Siri, and Google has its Voice Search, which is comparably great, and free to anyone who owns a Nexus 10.

The first time I played with it, I expected Voice Search to be rough around the edges, but I was consistently shocked by its depth and level of refinement. In its current incarnation, you ask a question in plain English and Voice Search tries to give you the definitive answer. If you know anything about the complexities of English syntax, you'll be blown away by the kinds of searches Voice Search can understand—as well as its uncanny ability to hunt down exactly the piece of information you're seeking.

When you first try Voice Search, your natural inclination will be

73

to test its limits. I expected it to know the easy stuff, like, "What is the United States population?" And of course it does.

But then you start ramping up the complexity of the questions, and Voice Search rarely falters:

"What year was Charles Dickens born?"

It knew.

"What team did Babe Ruth play for?"

Knew that one too.

"Who directed 2001: A Space Odyssey?"

Again, Voice Search had the answer at hand.

How about, "Who wrote *For Whom the Bell Tolls*?"

Hemingway, of course. The thing knows sports, movies, and literature. This was getting ridiculous. So I decided to do my level best to stump it:

"Where did Jim Morrison go to college?"

UCLA and Florida State University.

You've got to be kidding me.

I wasn't dumped into some lengthy Wikipedia page for each of these answers, where it was my job to pluck out the piece of data I needed. No, Voice Search brought up a single-sentence answer for each question, offering the answer and no extraneous information. What's more, the answers were accompanied by excellent portrait shots of Dickens, Ruth, Kubrick, Hemingway, and Morrison.

Chances are, if there's a request you can make, Google's engineers have anticipated it:

"Amazon.com stock price?" Or, perhaps, "What's 28 times 342?"

Check and check.

"Where is the Real Food Daily in Pasadena?"

A map showing Real Food Daily's Pasadena location comes right up.

How about, "Where is the nearest Costco?"

You're taken straight into Android's Maps app, where you'll receive driving directions (I wish it instead took you to the Navigation app, so you could just hop into your car and receive turn-by-turn spoken directions).

Can you stump Voice Search with an easy question? Absolutely. My question for "Final Score, Super Bowl 42" gave me a conventional Google Search results page, topped by a Wikipedia entry for that game that had the score prominently displayed. Consider that kind of response to be the sort of low-hanging fruit that Google hasn't gotten around to picking, but will undoubtedly get to soon.

Given that Voice Search is cloud-based, and that Google is undoubtedly pouring millions of dollars a month into improving the service, holes like a Super Bowl's final score are going to get smaller and harder to find. It wouldn't at all surprise me if by the time you're reading this, Google has created custom results pages for any basic Super Bowl question you could ask.

Using Voice Search as a Personal Assistant

With all that Voice Search has going for it, the software makes no attempt to duplicate the personal assistant functionality of Apple's Siri. With Siri, you can say, "Schedule a phone call with Scott on Wednesday at 2:00 PM," and Siri will add your event with Scott to Apple's Calendar app. Siri can likewise put through your call if you say, "Telephone Steven Perkins" and Steve is already listed in Apple's Contacts app.

But if you try requests like these in Google's personal assistant, you'll whiff.

It's not that Google's team hasn't anticipated these needs; a smart monkey could have seen everybody would want to do this sort of thing. In fact, somewhere in Google's Mountain View headquarters there's doubtless a version of Voice Search capable of doing all this and more. The trouble is that Apple and Google are currently battling it out in court regarding patents for these sorts of spoken requests. And, at the moment, Apple has the upper hand.

Software patents are one of those disgusting things that work against the public's best interest. It's been clear for decades that one day computers would have the voice recognition and interpretive capacities to do our bidding on any number of tasks. But Apple managed to get some key patents in this strategic area, and the company is not above using these patents to lock out competitors.

So, for now, Nexus 10 users are left without a Voice Search capable of performing some simple but important tasks. No doubt, however, if Google prevails in court they'll instantly release a version of Voice Search that's every bit as capable as Siri when it comes to acting as a personal assistant. Already it's more than a match for Siri in many key areas, and it's one of the coolest and most useful things to play with on your Nexus 10.

Chapter 12

Accessories

Thanks to the Nexus 10 having a micro-USB port, bluetooth, a headphone jack, magnetic sensor, and GPS receiver you can extend your tablet's capacities in any number of ways. This chapter rounds up some of the best Nexus 10 accessories on the market.

Protective Case

I own both a Nexus 7 and a Nexus 10, and they both get a ton of use. Since the Nexus 7 can do almost everything a Nexus 10 can do, my Nexus 10 seldom leaves the house. It's just a lot easier to bring my Nexus 7 with me if I'm going someplace, and I'm a lot more willing to risk travel damage to a $199 tablet than to a $399 tablet.

Because I'm frequently on the go with my Nexus 7, I own and recommend a RooCase Vegan Leather Folio Case Cover. It's fantastic, and gives my Nexus all the protection I need. I'll often wrap it with a rubber band to keep the cover shut if I'm carrying my Nexus in a bag or suitcase.

About the only time my Nexus 10 leaves the house is for lengthy trips out of town. Given that the Nexus 10 is already a large tablet, I don't want to bulk it up any further with a folio-style case. Instead, I recommend getting an inexpensive 10" netbook carrying pouch.

CaseCrown makes nice neoprene netbook cases that can be had on Amazon.com for $10 or less. These are perfect for keeping large tablets like the Nexus 10 protected in your suitcase.

USB Adapters

Your Nexus 10 comes with a micro-USB port. You'll therefore need an adapter if you want to connect your tablet to a USB keyboard or other device. The model I bought from Amazon.com was a Sanoxy USB 2.0 Female to Micro USB Male OTG Cable Adapter. It cost a whopping $1.27 with free shipping included.

Whatever brand of adapter you get, be sure it's labeled OTG (On the Go)—that way, it'll be compatible with USB thumb drives if you root your Nexus 10 or if Google ever decides to allow Android to access external storage over USB.

USB Keyboard

If you're only going to use a keyboard on rare occasions, save yourself some hassle and buy the adapter mentioned above plus a USB keyboard. And since, in this situation, you won't be using your keyboard much I'd recommend either a cheap Logitech or Microsoft keyboard. Both companies make excellent inexpensive USB keyboards.

You can't go wrong with the Logitech K120 or the Microsoft Wired Keyboard 600. Either can be purchased for under $15.

Bluetooth Keyboard

If you want to regularly use a keyboard with your Nexus 10, consider splurging for a bluetooth wireless unit. Whatever keyboard you buy, be sure that it's labeled bluetooth and not simply wireless, since the latter style of keyboards operates on a frequency incompatible with your Nexus 10.

Bluetooth keyboards aren't cheap. They start at about $30 for off-brand plastic ones. I recommend shelling out the $70 that Apple charges for its Bluetooth keyboard. It's a work of art, and solid beyond belief. You'll need some AA batteries to go with it. You might as well drop another $30 on the Apple battery charger, which comes with six AA NiMH batteries.

Tablet Stand

If you decide to get a keyboard, you're going to need a tablet stand to go with it. I recommend the Arkon Portable Fold-Up Stand. It's not the most attractive stand on the market, but it's the sturdiest, and will let you work with a large tablet like the Nexus 10 without any wobble.

Speakers (Bluetooth or Wired)

Through Bluetooth, you can listen to audio at a decent volume without your tablet being tethered to your speakers. Bluetooth-equipped speakers are surprisingly affordable—Creative's D80 unit costs less than $50 and gives you enough volume to listen comfortably to music and podcasts. And both Creative and Logitech make higher-end Bluetooth models that have a lot more fidelity.

If you don't do other things on your Nexus 10 while you're listening to audio, you may prefer a wired solution. A 3.5mm mini headphone to RCA stereo audio cable will enable you to plug your Nexus 10 into a stereo anytime you want. You can leave the cable plugged into your stereo, and plug the headphone jack into your Nexus 10 whenever you wish.

You could also get a nice bookshelf-appropriate pair of speakers that are intended for computers. JBL's Duet series is a quality brand of small, inexpensive speakers. On the higher end, consider Harman Kardon Soundsticks (Model III 2.1), which have a striking design and feature a subwoofer capable of filling a large room with music.

Micro HDMI to HDMI Cable

Get one of these and you'll be able to output the video from your Nexus 10 to any HDMI-equipped TV or computer display.

Chapter 13

Notifications

Sometimes your Nexus 10 needs to tell you something. Maybe you have successfully downloaded a file, or someone has just left you a text message over Google Talk, or you've got a calendar reminder for today. Given that you may in the middle of playing a game of Zen Pinball, how is your tablet supposed to bring these sorts of things to your attention?

That's where Android's Notification Panel comes in. Slide your finger down from the very top of the screen and it'll drag open a Notification Panel. In the panel, you'll be able to see all of your recent notifications.

You can touch a given item to open it. For instance, if you've received a voicemail message, you can select that item in the Notification Panel to listen to it.

If you want to delete any notification items, just swipe right on each item.

How do know if you've got anything waiting in the Notifications Panel? Just look at the top left corner of your Home screen. You'll see tiny icons representing any pending notifications.

Chapter 14

Mastering Your Email

Now that you own a Nexus 10, and have thereby gained unfettered access to Google's ecosystem of services, you've never been better equipped to take control of your email. Since email plays such a big part in all of our lives, and since most people adopt counterproductive strategies for managing it, I want to share my thoughts on how to get the most out of your Gmail account.

Ever since email became popular, there has been a relatively tiny group of people—computer networking geeks—who've had a virtually perfect experience with it. And then there has been the rest of us—deluged by spam and unwanted list email, we often turn to multiple email accounts in an attempt to retain our sanity.

Why is it that the geeks alone have enjoyed such a fundamentally better email experience? Because they have the specialized knowledge needed to set up and maintain a home email server. Anyone with the time and ability to operate a home server can easily install robust anti-spam filters and other technologies that make email the hassle-free experience that it's meant to be.

For the rest of us, well, you know the story as well as I do. Most Americans have two or more email accounts. We try to have one primary account for our friends, family, and co-workers that we jealously guard and hope the spammers never find out about. And then we establish one or more secondary accounts for our online purchases, email lists, forum memberships, and so forth.

In practice, we end up getting relevant email to all of these accounts. So we are stuck having to check all of our accounts regularly, often wading through a sea of spam and unwanted emails in the process.

But thanks to Google, there is a better way—the playing field has at long last been leveled so that non-technical people can enjoy the same quality of email experience as the geekiest of geeks. Best of all, there's no added cost to gaining these benefits. So why are most people still stuck in the email dark ages? The reason is simple. People don't yet realize that a single Gmail account can be perfectly configured to handle all of your email.

Let me get more specific about what I'm promising. If you follow the simple advice I offer in this chapter your email experience will transform in three ways:

1. Spam will disappear from your life.

2. You'll have just one email account, so all your email will go to the same place. No more checking and wading through multiple email accounts!

3. All those annoying list emails that you never subscribed to will vanish.

I hope you're excited about what I'm promising, so let's move on to how to make all this happen. I'll start with a plain vanilla solution that will be appropriate for most people, and then I'll introduce a couple other possibilities that should satisfy the needs of just about everyone else.

Gmail

When Gmail was first introduced, it wasn't much different from Hotmail, Yahoo Mail, and all the other free web services. Gmail offered more storage and a slicker interface, but its feature set wasn't noticeably superior to the competition.

But over time, Gmail has rolled out one upgrade after another. Today, anyone can take advantage of these combined features to attain email nirvana. So your first step to the promised land is to get a Gmail address, and to make this your primary account. The payoff will be immediate.

What if you want to receive email at a custom domain name? No problem. If you own HonestSamPlumbers.com, you can set Gmail up so that you're Sam@HonestSamPlumbers.com. For details and to get started, just visit:

```
http://www.google.com/a/
```

One of the many things that makes Gmail special is that its antispam technology far surpasses the competition. I used Hotmail and Yahoo Mail accounts for years, but neither company ever perfected their spam filters. Until I gave them up, my Hotmail and Yahoo inboxes were constantly cluttered with spam. Gmail, by contrast, approaches perfection where overcoming spam is concerned. I've used Gmail as my primary email account since 2005, and weeks at a time go by without my encountering a single piece of spam.

So, already, we see that the switch to Gmail has delivered on this article's first promise: spam will disappear from your life.

Set Up Auto-Forwarding from Your Other Accounts

Now it's time to move onto my second promise: that you can do away with all your other email accounts and check only Gmail. Over a period of years, the time you'll save by checking just one account is enormous. What's more, sooner or later you'll get burned by relying on secondary accounts.

Back in 2007, before I enacted the advice I'm giving here, I put in an order for a banner for a convention exhibit I was sponsoring.

Since I didn't want to risk being added to an email list, I gave the banner company my secondary Hotmail address, which I only bothered to check a couple times a month. A few days after I placed my order, they emailed me back at that address saying they couldn't move forward with creating my banner until I approved the design. But since I didn't know that this email had arrived, things slipped past the deadline before I gave my OK, and I didn't receive my banner in time for the convention.

So here's how to drive all your emails to your Gmail account. If your secondary email accounts support auto-forwarding, just set them up to have all email forwarded to your Gmail account. Gmail will automatically filter out any spam you receive from these accounts, and any responses you make to correspondence from your secondary accounts will go out with your new Gmail address. Note that some webmail providers may charge for auto-forwarding. So if you don't want to pay for auto-forwarding from an account you intend to stop using, you'll need to email the important contacts you've corresponded with from your previous account and notify them of your new Gmail address. You should also unsubscribe from any email lists that point to your secondary accounts, and then re-subscribe using your Gmail address.

If you've got important contact information saved in the address books of your alternate accounts, it's usually easy to import that information into Gmail. Most webmail services allow you to export your address book. Then (on your desktop or laptop) go to Gmail's contacts section, click the *More* button (the *More* button immediately above your list of contacts, not the one in the navigation bar), and select *Import...* from the popup menu. You could also import contact files on your Nexus 10 through its People app, but this is exactly the sort of task that's easier done on a Mac or PC than a tablet.

Once you've imported all your contacts, you'll be two-thirds of the way towards attaining the perfect email setup: You'll have a single address where all your email goes, and you'll have virtually zero spam.

Dealing with List Mail from Distant Acquaintances

At this point, you may have some doubts about the advice I've offered. Does the idea of funneling all your secondary account emails to Gmail sound worrisome? Won't you end up with tons of unwanted crud in your precious Gmail account? Nope.

Your Gmail account will in fact stay cleaner than you could ever imagine, if you follow my final piece of advice: you've got to make appropriate use of Gmail's filter feature. It's super easy, and as we'll see, incredibly satisfying to use this feature. In order to explain this feature, I need to talk about my general philosophy about what email is for—and what it's not for. By way of introduction, let me tell you a quick story about my own transition to email nirvana.

Five minutes after I switched my primary account to Gmail and followed the steps I've just laid out, I received a piece of forwarded email from one of my secondary accounts. To avoid publicly embarrassing this person, I'll use a made-up name here: "David J. Gold." The name was one I recalled from past emails but I didn't quite remember if we had met at some point, or if we had corresponded.

Most of my daily work involves animal advocacy, and this email from Mr. Gold was a BCC (blind carbon copy) sent to who knows how many other people. The topic of this email pertained to an aspect of animal protection that's outside of my focus, and of no interest to me whatsoever. I had no idea why on earth Mr. Gold sent me this email. He didn't write me a personal note explaining why—he just inconsiderately lumped me in with his other BCCs. Emails like Mr. Gold's are infinitely worse than spam. You know at a glance that any email with Viagra in the title is spam and need not be opened. But emails from someone you've vaguely heard of with a relevant-sounding subject line demand a quick read, on the chance they contain something of value.

I became curious about my history with Mr. Gold, so I performed a search of my secondary account to bring up all our past correspondence. I discovered that over the past three years Mr. Gold had sent me about thirty other BCCs, all completely irrelevant to me and all a waste of time. But you know what? It turned out that I had opened every single one of these worthless BCCs, read them quickly, and had to expend mental energy deciding to ignore them.

Coming in only every month or so, David J. Gold's emails never quite rose to the level that I was conscious of the source of this regular annoyance. Through these infrequent and unrequested missives, Mr. Gold managed to interrupt me thirty times in three years, demand some of my attention, while giving me nothing of value. Only once did I write back to him—and that was when I read one of his emails advertising a picnic occurring 2000 miles from my house. I asked him to take me off his list. He didn't respond, but he was back a month later with yet another of his irrelevant BCCs.

The reason David J. Gold managed to persistently abuse my inbox for three years was that his emails were being sent to one of my secondary accounts. These accounts were perpetually awash with irrelevant list-based email, and I never took action against abuse.

But now that I check only my Gmail account, I'm much zealous about defending this solitary account from unwanted emails. Happily, the version of Gmail that runs on Macs and PCs provides a quick and easy way to rigorously defend my inbox: the "Filter" button (the option to add or remove filters is not yet available on the Nexus 10's Gmail app).

Not only are filters incredibly effective, they're also satisfying and fun to use. Here's how they work: anytime you receive a list email from some bozo who is abusing your email address, just open that email and then click on the *More Actions* pulldown menu and select *Filter messages like these.* Once the filter screen opens, choose the *Delete it* checkbox to block that person's emails from ever reaching you again.

Now, obviously, I'm not suggesting you block your mother, your best friend, or a business contact. In my experience, none of the people close to me are clueless enough to send David J. Gold style emails. But if they were, I would write to them and tell them that I only receive personal email at my address.

Once you adopt a single inbox approach, you're likely to discover that nearly all the email abuse you've been suffering comes from a tiny number of David J. Golds—people you've never met nor corresponded with in any meaningful way, but who somehow think that you're eager to read their bulk emails. As we've seen, a single mouse click within Gmail on the Mac or PC puts a stop to all this abuse.

Now that we've seen how to banish the people who abuse your inbox, let me put the utility of email into context. Understanding the strengths and weaknesses of email is key to getting the most out of your inbox.

Email vs. Feeds

Email is probably the best *correspondence* tool ever invented, but it is a miserable *broadcasting* tool. It's often a poor choice for both broadcaster and recipient alike. In fact, email broadcasting persists mainly because the majority of people haven't yet caught on to a superior technology intended specifically for broadcasting: RSS Feeds.

RSS Feeds correct everything that's wrong with using email for broadcasting. Once you switch to RSS, your email box will never be cluttered with list mail. Spam filters—even Google's!—tend to shoot down some legitimate list mail, but if you subscribe to a feed with an RSS reader you'll never miss an item.

By its design, RSS prevents inbox clutter and overload. Nobody would want to be on a mailing list that sends ten different emails a day; the resultant inbox clutter would be unmanageable. But RSS readers are built to gracefully handle and automatically organize incoming messages, whether the feed in question publishes new material once a month or fifty.times a day. For more on RSS readers, please see Chapter 9.

If you must subscribe to an email list, I urge you to set up a Gmail filter for high-volume lists so those emails get routed to a secondary folder rather than to your inbox. That way you won't have list emails and personal emails dumped into the same place.

To sum up: the best way to stay current in your areas of interest is by subscribing to RSS feeds, not email lists. No matter what your interest, whether it's volleyball or anti-hunger activism or particle physics, there are superb RSS feeds available for you to subscribe to. The days of keeping informed by wading through a barrage of list emails flooding your inbox are over.

The Attention Economy

Let's now return to the main subject of this chapter: maintaining the sanctity of your inbox. There is more to be learned from my encounter with David J. Gold.

Nobody wants to feel overwhelmed by unsolicited email. Happily, unless you're Lady Gaga or Justin Bieber, the number of unknown people who will contact you is usually quite manageable. I've sold 50,000 books and publish a high-traffic website, yet I probably get only one or two emails a day from strangers. As long as the unsolicited email I receive is polite and reasonable, I'll always take a minute to respond.

But I don't have time for people who are nasty, clueless, or disrespectful of my time. And one of the main benefits of having only one email account is it encourages you to be vigilant when people are abusive of your time and goodwill.

Until recently, if a stranger added me to an unwanted email list, and there was no footer offering a link to unsubscribe, I would send a short and polite response asking to be removed from the list. Almost invariably, I would get a nasty and defensive email back, and the unsettling knowledge that I had created one more antagonist in my world. I now believe that the best way to handle the David J. Golds of your inbox is to put a stop to the abuse and not create any ill-will. The sender has already abused your time and proven himself clueless about email etiquette, so you owe him nothing. Just click the Gmail filter button and you'll never hear from him again. I can't begin to tell you how satisfying this is.

It turns out that a tiny number of clueless people account for the overwhelming majority of unwanted emails that clutter your inbox. Judicious use of Gmail's filter button will therefore quickly turn the overall quality of your inbox from bronze into gold.

When I've described my filtering practices to friends, some have protested that I might lose something important. That's a risk I'm prepared to take. If you give the matter some thought, I bet you'll agree that anyone who is too clueless to catch on to basic email etiquette has proven themselves unworthy of your continued attention. Make good use of Gmail's filter button and never again will you have to deal with a stream of unsolicited emails.

My approach regarding making myself available for strangers to contact me is simple. My time is precious, and it is a privilege to contact me—a privilege I'm delighted to extend to anyone who doesn't abuse my inbox. But the moment my generosity is abused, I permanently revoke this privilege by clicking Gmail's filter button. My inbox is available to seven billion people in the world, but it is closed to strangers who add me to email lists without my consent or who lack basic social skills. If you take the advice in this paragraph to heart, I believe it will profoundly enhance your experience with email.

It never occurred to me that Thoreau's maxim of "simplify, simplify, simplify" could be brought to email. But now, I feel like I've won the lottery. Spam has vanished from my life. I have only one email account to check. And reading my email no longer means frustrating encounters with the likes of David J. Gold.

Gmail has always been an excellent webmail provider, but few of its users are fully acquainted with its marvelous feature set. If you take advantage of the features and strategies described in this chapter, and begin shifting your email subscriptions to RSS, your email experience will rise to an entirely new level. For the first time, anyone can attain email nirvana, with no investment of time or money, and no advanced technical skills required.

Chapter 15

Troubleshooting

This book was never intended to be a step-by-step guide to using a Nexus 10. Rather, its purpose was to help you discover the enormous range of possibilities for using the Nexus 10 to enhance your life. I hope I've succeeded.

That said, I can't in good conscience finish this book without offering a couple pieces of advice in case you run into trouble. Just like an iPad, the Nexus 10 will occasionally act up. You'll find an app that stalls, or won't properly open, or won't do what it's supposed to do. And just like an iPad, the first thing to try when problems appear is to reboot your tablet. With your Nexus 10 already turned on, just press the power button and hold it down for a second and then touch the *Power off* menu option that will appear on your screen.

One of the many things the iPad and Nexus 10 share is that when you turn them off, you're actually just putting them to sleep. You're cutting most of the power but the tablet is really just hibernating. Once it's turned back on, there's no need for the system to reboot— which is why both the iPad and Nexus 10 immediately spring to life when you hit the power button.

But when you reboot a Nexus 10 or iPad you shut down your tablet completely. The next time it's powered on, it must go through the elaborate procedure of reloading the operating system. While this rebooting takes less than a minute, it can work miracles. You've essentially wiped the slate clean of any weirdness that may be causing unwanted behavior from Android or your apps. So rebooting is always the first thing to try when you run into any sort of crashing or unwanted behavior from your Nexus 10. Rebooting never hurts, and it generally solves the problem.

Of course, problems may arise that rebooting can't solve. Sometimes it's a bug in your app, and sometimes the trouble is that you don't understand the app's design well enough. Either way, it's rare that you'll encounter a problem that other people haven't experienced as well. And it's amazing how often a well-constructed Google search (which names both the app and the problem) will point to a solution.

If you're pretty sure that you've run into an actual software bug, visit the app developer's website to see if there's a solution. Larger software companies will often maintain a forum website where you can see if other users of your app have had similar complaints. Most software companies are eager to receive bug reports and will quickly respond to an email.

There's no need to bang your head against the wall if you've encountered a software problem that rebooting won't fix. Most of the time, the solution to your problem is already out there, and a quick online search will reveal an easy fix that will get you on your way.

NexusGuides.com

I am grateful that you picked up this book, and I hope you've found it helpful. I also publish an email newsletter and produce videos that will help you get the most out of your Nexus 10. To access this material, just visit NexusGuides.com.

If you've benefited from reading this book, I'd greatly appreciate your posting a review to Amazon.com or the Google Play store. And if there's anything about this book that fell short of your expectations, please shoot an email to me at Erik@NexusGuides.com.